Quails as Pets

Quail Owner's Manual

Quail keeping pros and cons, care, housing, diet and health.

By

Roger Rodendale

Contents

Table of Contents

Table of Contents

Introduction

The idea of domesticating animals is not new; we have been creating a chain of connections with several species in the animal kingdom for the purpose of peaceful coexistence. History may have taught modern man to breed cattle, horses and poultry for personal consumption and trade; our relationship with animals today, however, has become more complex, even emotional.

We now view animals, not only as a source of self-sustenance, but also as a source of profit, and even companionship. Through our discovery of new species and their natures, we have also modified the concept of domestication, with exotic species being domesticated with as much enthusiasm - and considerable success - as the conventional ones. Some other commonly domesticated animals and poultry from the older civilizations, on the other hand, have found a resurgence in the husbandry market, due their valuable produce - whether through hide, meat or eggs. What is fascinating, however, is that people tend to have varied preferences when asked to select an animal they would prefer to raise.

For some, the perfect animal companion is one that is energetic, affectionate and boisterous. Those with a quiet demeanor may prefer an animal that is well-behaved, disciplined and calm. Some may describe their perfect companions to be those who swim behind large glass enclosures, providing tranquillity and beauty. And some others still may choose to bring home those pets that can be raised for long-term profits and exhibition. If you belong to that industrious group of people who seek the company of animals that require less care, handling and attention but have high yield value, Quail may be the ideal pets for you.

Of the over 130 species of Quail that are found around the world, only a handful have been observed to be suitable for husbandry and domestication. The limit posed by Wildlife and Game laws and the aversion towards domestication displayed by many New World Quail breeds makes it additionally challenging to house and rear just about any breed available. After a prolonged history of exposure to humans, however, Coturnix Quail found in Asian and European countries, along with some varieties of the Bobwhite, Mountain and Gambel's Quail - to name a few - found in the North American continent have either been studied or bred to be most suitable for taming and husbandry.

Curious and energetic by nature, these members of the bird family prefer to spend their existence engaging in foraging and egg-laying behaviors while in captivity, with some hours of the day devoted towards grooming and rest. Despite their curious natures, several breeds of Quail, particularly those from the Callipepla and Colinus families, display an aversion towards being handled for long periods of time, and will responds by attempting to run, hide or even fly.

A quality that makes the Quail - regardless of its breed - a prized pet is its ability to be of great production value, if given proper care and attention. Provided it is housed in a safe enclosure that promotes egg-laying and healthy mating, receives plenty of food for immediate feeding and protection from predators and infections, your Quail will live a content life of up to 5 years. In the course providing you with meat, eggs, or an elite status as an owner of a strikingly beautiful bird.

These omnivorous creatures have healthy appetites, but require relatively less feed per day when compared to other animals intended for husbandry, such as chickens. They are also prone to bursts of aggression and hostility during the breeding season, and may become aggressive towards each other in order to secure a mate or protect the eggs from the rest of the flock. On the flip side, those Quail who are comfortable around humans, especially the Coturnix breeds, also make for sociable companions that are content to feed from the hands of those caregivers they trust.

This family of birds are also of robust health, rarely succumbing to the communicable, life-threatening illnesses that plague other poultry breeds, such as chickens, turkeys or Quails.. Common health-related ailments may include superficial wounds and injuries sustained during fights, infections contracted due to inhospitable and unhygienic housing conditions, or as a result of a nutritional deficiency through an improper diet.

The health and well-being of Quail in captivity is largely reliant on the kind of living environment you can provide; different breeds will require slight variations in housing and interaction. In favorable and nurturing environments, Quail can also be extremely easy and rewarding to breed, whether for personal use or for profit. From breeding Quail for their eggs and meat, to experimenting with cross-breeding to find new coloring patterns, breeding Quail has become a passion among several enthusiasts. It is no wonder, then, that Quail are enthusiastically given a home by anyone who is lucky - or enterprising enough - to house some of these.

If you, too, wish to bring home Quail, through this book, you will gain deeper insight into its world - from its natural settings, to its behavioral patterns. You will also be guided through every stage of owning Quail, from initial thought to eventual raising for profit or personal companionship. With a positive attitude and a dedicated spirit, you can work past the challenges that come with housing Quail, and make them a positive and transformative part of your life.

Chapter 1: Know your Quail

1. The Relationship between Quail and Humans

With small, rounded bodies that provide nutrition and energy through meat and eggs, quail have been reared and farmed for their domestic value for over 4,000 years. So ancient is their relationship with human beings, that experts have found hieroglyphs with symbols for the quail around ancient Egyptian sites. A study of the Biblical texts will also reveal numerous mentions of quail as a source of food – especially through times of strife.

Early Egyptian civilization records, in fact, state the benefits of the meat and eggs of the quail as food for laborers. High in energy, minerals and vitamins, yet low in cholesterol, quail meat provided more strength and endurance to the laborers at a cheaper rate than other meats. Quail farms themselves were simple, small and relatively inexpensive to maintain; making this bird the chief source of nutrition among the common working class.

Similar uses for quail meat and eggs have been documented in texts uncovered during early European civilizations as well. Curiously, this copious documentation of the benefits of quail farming, while found in abundantly in both the Egyptian and European excavation sites, have rarely pointed towards actual quail farm locations within these civilizations.

Across the world, in early China and Japan, however, historians and experts have discovered that quail have enjoyed a more revered status among these civilizations. Through various documents, quail farm locations, and mentioned in the local literature and art, it is evident that not only were quail farmed for nutrition, but also for their value as personal companions.

Through research, it has been uncovered that quail may have been farmed in China and Japan as early as 770 BC; indeed, the Chinese quail is arguably considered to be the first member in the lineage of several quail breeds today. Found extensively in Japan, quail were taken across the land to China in the 11th century, where they became prized for their unique singing voice, and found a place in many a parlour.

In Japan itself, documentation on quail farming dates back as early as the 12th century, while also stressing on the medicinal and therapeutic benefits of the bird's meat. Chiefly petted and consumed by the royal family at first, quail farming is said to have gained fame among the lower echelons of society when the Emperor was believed to have been cured from an acute case of Tuberculosis after subsisting on a quail meat diet for a few days.

It is perhaps this belief in the high medicinal value of the quail that has turned it into an occupation that has survived multiple centuries. The Japanese quail, today, is considered to be an ideal bird for farming and domestication, thanks to millennia of interaction with human beings lending it a social disposition. With a significant section of the population in China and Japan still engaged in quail rearing, this practice has also become common in such countries as India and other parts of south-east and central Asia.

With the passage of time and the need for sustainable and cheap sources of protein and nutrition, the Coturnix quail, owing to its hardy and robust nature, found itself transported across continents, reaching Europe and eventually the Americas. Its descendants, such as the Texas A&M, the Tuxedo and the Rosetta, among other breeds, have been engineered to produce not only a higher quantity of eggs per year, but also to have a varied array of physical coats in hues ranging from white and brown to shades of rusty red and black.

Such quail breeds native to the Americas as the Bobwhite Quail, Gambel's Quail and the California Quail were found to also be excellent game for hunting expeditions favoured by the people in the 1800s. The California Quail, in particular, gained such infamy as the game bird of choice that it was shipped off to such lands as Hawaii, Europe, and even New Zealand. Not commonly hunted for sport any longer, the California quail, apart from enjoying its status as the state bird of California, has also been immortalized through appearances in such classic animated features as Disney's Bambi.

While urbanization and excessive hunting operations may have greatly reduced the numbers of many indigenous quails in the North American continent over the years, commercial quail farming and husbandry has now made it possible for several of the quail breeds not only survive, but also thrive.

2. Natural Range and Habitat

The ability to adapt with ease to a variety of conditions is probably why Quail are arguably among the oldest of all domesticated animal species. This resilience to accept a diverse range of climate conditions, food and terrains has helped Quail thrive in both the Northern as well as the Southern Hemispheres.

In the Americas, you're most likely to find Quail in abundance from Central Alaska all the way down to Mexico, including such states as California, Utah, Texas and New Mexico. The Caribbean region, though located a considerable distance away from the United States, also boasts of a healthy Quail population including those species that were introduced to the islands form the American continent.

Across the ocean, Quail continue to comfortably inhabit the vast expanse of the Eurasian region. In the northern Hemisphere, expect to see lots of Quail in the United Kingdom and sometimes

11

in Turkey. As we move eastwards, Quail once again become abundant in East Asia, in Japan, China, India and Russia. During the winter months, the Quail have been observed to sometimes move southwards towards Korea.

Quail have also shown a fondness for the mildly tropical climates of the African region, especially during the winter months; Tanzanina, Malawi, Egypt and the region surrounding the Nile Valley boasts of a large population of Quail during the latter months of the year. And further still, Quail have made their homes in the southern regions of Australia and New Zealand, either through migration or through introduction to the continent by early human visitors.

3.   Living Conditions

It seems fairly clear by now that Quail will find a way to adapt to nearly any variation that location, climate and food sources may throw at them. This doesn't mean that Quail don't have living preferences, simply that they are not particularly fussy.

Even though Quail inhabit a wide variety of spaces, it is the dry, grassy lands with plenty of space to forage and hide that they show the highest preference for. As long as their immediate surroundings are not too wet or covered with excessively deep water bodies, many breeds of Quail are perfectly content as ground-dwelling species along the shallow banks of rivers, fields, meadows and the slightly inaccessible mountainous terrain close to a shallow water source.

Perhaps the only prerequisite that Quail look for before settling in is the depth of the surrounding water body. Their preferred settlements mostly comprise of waters that measure less than a meter. Aside from this one determining factor, as long as a location contains a sustainable food source, a water body and some level of privacy, you can expect a flock of Quail to make it their home.

4.   Quail and the Ecology

Quail have managed to carve a unique existential zone within the ecology, thanks to their choice of habitat and feeding habits. Within the vast ecological space, Quail find themselves categorized with their medium-sized counterparts that live in terrestrial conditions. In addition, Quail further slot themselves into a niche by being ground-dwelling birds of medium-size who are also omnivorous in nature. Within these parameters, however, quail find themselves contributing significantly to the ecological cycle.

As is the law of nature, Quail, like all other living beings, play several direct and indirect roles to help maintain ecological balance. One of their most significant roles is perhaps their contribution towards seed dispersal. Taken in through their feed and shed through their droppings, the Quail's preference for grains and seeds allows the seeds in their droppings to travel along water banks and air pollination and plant themselves across a wider area. The Quails also allow for seeds dispersal through droppings when in flight.

It is not only the spread of seeds, but also the control of unwanted plants that Quail can claim responsibility for. Their fondness for pecking on wild grasses and weeds in their surroundings helps healthy plants thrive without any competition for food and light sources.

Quail also carry out this balancing act in the insect kingdom. By feeding on a steady supply of a variety of insects, this breed of Quails helps to maintain a regulated number of insects in an ecosystem. In fact, many personal accounts of Quail post-mortem dissections have claimed their throats to be filled with insects of the winged variety - mosquitoes, flies, beetles etc.

The medium-sized bodies of the Quail help them escape the eyes of a number of predators along the food chain. They still, however, are an easy enough feeding target for such land animals as domestic and wild dogs, along with foxes or coyotes present in the same areas. While there have been observations of canine predators chasing adult Quails for food, coyotes, foxes and dogs have largely shown a preference for the easier-to-acquire eggs and hatchlings.

This doesn't mean that adult Quail are safe from the eyes of predators; aviary predators have shown special fondness for adult Quail. This makes them obvious targets for such birds of prey as hawks, falcons and eagles, and even others, likes magpies and crows.

Apart from these naturally selected predators, Quail now also have human beings to contend with. An increasingly popular form of poultry in many parts of the world, the use of Quail as a food source could be an explanation for their depleting number in certain areas such as Mexico.

Chapter 2: Understand your Quail

1. Physical Traits and Appearance

An adult Quail usually grows to a length between 22 to 28 cms in length and 30 to 38 cms in wingspan, settling in at a weight in the range of 100 and 200 gms, reaching even 300 gms in weight in captive conditions. A healthy adult Quail is often classified by the above optimum length, weight and wingspan, along with three other important physical traits. A bill that is short and curved, along with a distinctively colored plumage with coloring across the neck, throat and feathers are what characterize a healthy Quail, whether male or female.

It has been noticed that male Quail grow to a size smaller than their female counterparts; they do, however, possess a more striking plumage to help attract females during the mating ritual. While possessing the same features as developing chicks, Quail male and female attain individual physical traits and characteristics up on attaining maturity; it is during this period that sexing male and female Quail becomes easier.

Whether among the Coturnix breeds or the Colinus breeds, the base coat of the adult quail will range from a pale brown to a blue-grey hue. It is the marking around the face, neck, and dorsal feathers that often tell the males apart from the females -

depending on the breeds, male Quail will have vibrantly colored markings in shades of black, rust, orange-to red and even blue when compared to the duller and splotched appearance of the adult female coat.

Quail have an average life expectancy of around 2 to 5 years in captivity, probably even less in the wild, with some domesticated Quail living slightly longer. As part of this considerably short lifespan, Quail develop fairly quickly, reaching full maturation and adulthood between the ages of 6 to 8 weeks.

2. Different Types of Quail

The following are some of the most popular types of Quail breeds, that are easily found and valued highly in the animal husbandry or exhibition market:

1. **Name:** Coturnix Quail
   Appearance: Males: Rusty orange throat and breast; Females: White speckled breast

   Size: Males: 100-140gms (4-5 oz.) Females: 120-160gms (4.5-6 oz.)

   Maturity: 7-9 weeks

   Life expectancy: 2-5 years

   Natural Range:

   Varieties: Jumbo, Texas A&M, Tuxedo, Rosetta, Tibetan, English White, Golden Coturnix

2. **Name:** Button Quail
   Appearance: Males: White or red line on throat, red or blue feathering; Females: Absence of red or blue feather coloring, no white line on throat

   Size: 1.5 oz. approx.

   Maturity: 8-12 weeks

16

Life expectancy: 3-5 years

Natural Range:

Varieties: Blue-faced, Red-breasted, White, Cinnamon Tuxedo Pied

3. **Name:** Bobwhite Quail
Appearance:

Size: 6-16 oz.

Maturity: 6 months - 1 year

Life expectancy: 2-5 years

Natural Range: United States, Caribbean, Mexico,

Varieties: Northern, Butler, Tennessee Red, Georgia Giant, Snowflake

4. **Name:** Gambel's
Appearance: Male: Black mask-like patterns on face, white stripes on back, rust colored face; Female: Brown face

Maturity: 6 months - 1 year

Life expectancy: 2-5 years

Natural Range: Arizona, New Mexico, Utah, Texas, Colorado and North Mexico

5. **Name:** California/Mountain
Appearance: Male: Brightly colored, more vibrant hue of grey with grey-blue head; Female: Shorter, brown plume with brown head

Size: 189-262 gms (6.7 - 9.2 oz.)

Maturity: 6 months - 1 year

Life expectancy: 2-5 years

Natural Range: California, Oregon, Nevada

6. **Name:** Montezuma
    Appearance: White head with black mask-patterns around face, speckled white and black/brown plumage

    Maturity: 6 months - 1 year

    Life expectancy: 8 months - 2 years

    Natural Range: United States, Mexico

7. **Name:** Blue Scale
    Appearance: Blue-grey and brown scaled plumage

    Maturity: 6 months - 1 year

    Life expectancy: 8 months - 2 years

    Natural Range: United States, Mexico

3.   Old World Quail versus New World Quail

Though the quail species may comprise over 130 different breeds in today's world, only a handful of members from this branch of the pheasant family can trace their roots back to the ancient Egyptian and Japanese civilization. Other breeds have had a limited amount of interaction with humans and the state of captivity, having been introduced as recently as a quarter-century ago.

This large time divide that separates some breeds of quail from the others on the basis of existence, has also been found to bring up other differences amongst them. Depending on the time of their introduction, factors such as physical characteristics, behavioral traits and easiness of domesticity are noticeably different among the breed's, leading experts to categorize quail into two broad groups – Old world quail and New world quail.

Old world Quail include the Coturnix Quail family of species that have been reared in domesticity for thousands of years. Such breeds as the Japanese Coturnix, the European and the Chinese Painted Button Quail are all examples of Old World breeds who formed the genetic code for the younger, newer members of the Quail family.

New World Quail generally include the Colinus family of Quail, among others, such as the Bobwhite branch of the Quail species. Introduced into the ecosystem several hundred years after their Coturnix cousins, New World Quail have experienced a limited amount of contact with other animals or humans, making them a suspicious and slightly hostile family of Quail.

This difference in behaviour towards other animals is perhaps the largest differentiating factor between Old and New World Quail. With a pleasing disposition inherited through generations of handling by humans, Old World Quail such as the Coturnix varieties are found to be easy to handle and care for. Such Breeds as the Bobwhite, on the other hand, are known to be more paranoid by nature, either hiding or taking off in flight as a response to unfamiliar situations.

A relatively large gap between the introduction of New and Old World species has also brought about a significant difference in their physical characteristics as well; New World species have been found to possess slightly larger bodies and broader breasts than their Old World counterparts; they are, however, also slightly more susceptible to infections and ailments from other poultry than the Old world Quail, owing to lower rate of overall immunity.

While the differences between the Old and New World species of Quail may not be that vast or striking; they do play an important part in determining which breeds are suitable for an amateur Quail farmer, depending on the behaviour patterns and physical appearance of the birds.

4. Quail and the Reproductive cycle

Depending on the breed of the Quail, come breeding time, the hen may either be monogamous and choose one partner, or may even choose two or more partners to fertilize her eggs. This selected cockerel will usually be the biggest in physical size, may have the most impressive plumage and crest, and may also be the most aggressive of the flock. It is such dominant behavior that makes a Quail drake attractive to sexually active females.

What is interesting to note, however, is that some Quail cockerels may not be content mating with just one female, as other breeds of the Quail family do. Staying true to their reputation of being prolific breeders, Coturnix Quail will impregnate multiple females over the course of their lives. Those Quail cockerels within the flock that are deemed unfit for mating, usually congregate to form their own sub-group - a flock of bachelors, if you will.

The act of mating itself is carried out when the cockerel mounts the female quail upon receiving her attention, and grabs her by the neck. If the female so wishes, she can just as easily attract the attention of her desired mate by simply crouching in front of the cockerel to present her availability. The cockerel then attempts to create cloacal contact by arching his back - an act that may appear aggressive and hostile, but in fact, is pleasurable to the female.

Upon insemination, Quail cockerel possess the curious and amusing habit of briefly strutting around the housing area almost as an act of boasting or pride. The female, on her part, will then lay the rest of the eggs within a few hours, generally before it turns dark. Once she has laid her eggs for the day, a Quail hen in the wild then proceeds to incubate her clutch for a period of around 16 days, with the eggs hatching on the 17th day.

The brooding period brings out the most aggressive behaviour among female Quail in the wild; many females tend to become aggressive not only towards other animals, but also towards their mates. Curiously, centuries of raising in captivity has made some types of Coturnix quail averse or indifferent to the concept of nesting and maybe even brooding altogether.

Domesticated Quail females, if conditioned, will replicate the art of nest-building in the wild by gathering soft materials available in their premises and setting it up in preferred corners. Once the nest is ready, the female lays an egg daily, till she has collected a batch of up to 10 eggs. Upon reaching her desired number, the female Quail stops laying further eggs and perches herself on the batch, providing warmth and incubation till the eggs hatch.

Quail eggs only begin the process of development and hatching when they receive the first bout of incubation; the female will avoid providing this warmth till she has laid her last egg. This act is the female Quails way of timing the birth of her hatchlings, which makes feeding and resting easier for the mother and the Quail as well.

During the brooding period, female Quail will leave their spots unattended for only an hour or so a day. They use this time to perform their daily ablutions, and maybe exercise their wings and feet. The eggs of Quail living in the wild or raised in open housing environment are most susceptible to predatory attacks during this time.

Provided the female Quail can safely incubate her eggs for an extended period, hatchlings will emerge from the eggs after about 16 to 18 days. The Quail first emerges by forming a tiny hole or "pip" in the shell. Chipping away at the eggshell with an especially formed calcified tip, Quailing will successfully break out of their shell after a few hours from the first crack.

While slightly wet as soon as burst from their shells, Quail will dry off fairly quickly, and will open their eyes almost instantly. Within a few hours, most hatchlings will have dried off completely, and begun to walk about unsteadily.

For the first few weeks, young hatchlings cannot provide enough warmth and sustenance for themselves, and are tended to by their mother. Over the course of these formative weeks, the mother also takes up the responsibility of introducing such concepts as foraging, feeding, drinking and bathing to her young ones. The reproductive cycle is then carried forward when the hatchlings mature into an adult flock and begin sexual activity during the nearest mating season.

It is also interesting to note that while the Quail are highly involved in the earlier stages of mating, they seldom participate in the construction of nests of the subsequent care that hatchlings require. These roles are generally limited to the female members of the flock alone.

5. Common behavioural patterns

Quail, depending on their breed, natural habitat, and level of interaction with other animals, possess a varied range of behavioral patterns that make them interesting to observe, both in the wild and in captivity. Common to all ground-dwelling birds, however, Quail are linked to each other through such common behaviors as foraging, nesting, and displaying aggression during the breeding and mating period.

Older Quail breeds such as the Japanese Coturnix or the California Quail have been studied to possess a sociable nature that encourage interaction with other members of their species. Preferring to exist and thrive in flocks also known as coveys, adult Quail share such duties as feeding, dust bathing and caring for the young. While some flocks may be small in size, the inherently interactive nature of Quail means that you can easily spot a covey of over 100 Quail, comprising both young and adults, at any point in the wild.

Dust bathing in particular, seems to be a preferred behavioral trait among several Quail species - not only has this practice found to be healthy for the upkeep of the bird's coat, but has also been observed to provide a deep sense of pleasure to the Quail themselves. So great is the pleasure derived during dust bathing rituals, which remnants of their activity can be spotted in pieces of soft earth, with indentations measuring up to 15 cms in diameter.

Another common behavior pattern shared by several species of Quail is the tendency to "flush" upwards in flight, in time of threat or fear. Owing to their small sizes, Quail will rarely attempt to confront their predators or sources of threat, choosing instead to evade capture by taking abrupt flight upwards. While a successful means of evasion in the wild, this startled reaction in a captive setting often proves fatal to the Quail's health.

Perhaps best known for their vocal abilities, Quail possess an intricate and complex range of vocalizations, with over 28 recorded sounds by ornithologists known to cover such situations as perceived threat, warning, arrival of food and mating. Made up of intricate tones of chirps, pips and squeaks, some Quail breeds, in fact, are famed for their antiphonal vocal prowess, and can stun their audience for hours on end by harmonizing their vocals with their life mate; this behavioural trait is especially true of the Chinese Painted Button Quail.

Communication patterns are often highly advanced among Quail; the young have known to send out distress calls and other warning signals to their parents to signify such activities as hatching of the eggs.

Other sensory systems, such as vision auditory perception and smell, are especially strong and complex among the Quail species; they are known to have the ability to spot tiny grains of food from great distances. Senses such as hearing and taste are equally sharp, while much is not yet known about the Quail's ability to smell.

6.   The shifting behaviours of Coturnix Quail

As a pure species, Coturnix Quail are among those birds who, in the wild, thrive by existing in large flocks or coveys, and distributing the parental duties with their mate. They are also birds who, in many instances have proven to be species who mate for life. Engaging in such duties as helping to build the brooding nest with some cockerels taking care of egg clutches that are not theirs, and nurturing the young long after they are born are also considered inherent traits of the Quail cockerel.

It is, perhaps, surprising then, to notice that several Coturnix Quail cockerel in the contemporary world, display a sense of ambiguity over their preference for a monogamous or polygamous lifestyle. When raised for profit or in captivity, both the cockerel, and the hen have been found to select more than one partner to mate with, may display overly aggressive behaviour towards other males in the cage, or may be completely indifferent towards their clutch. Curiously, New World Breeds and those Quail species such as the Bobwhite and Button Quail, are strictly monogamous and will rarely display polygamous behaviours.

While the true cause of the shifting nature of the Coturnix quail nesting and brooding behaviours is still being studied, this shift in parental priority has largely been attributed towards rearing in domesticity - a feature that absolves the Quail of hatching and incubating duties, placing them on a human owner. Their willingness to be conditioned to resume such parental behaviors could further support the argument that rearing Quail in domesticity may affect their parental instincts in the long run.

Chapter 3: The Quail as a Pet

1.   Initial investments and continued costs behind caring for Quail

The price of Quail cannot only be limited to calculating their individual costs. You also have to account for their initial housing expenses, feeding and bathing supplies, as well as health requirements. Depending on the scale of your endeavor, these costs may range from a few hundred pounds to tens of thousands.

It is often assumed that a pet as small a Quail will not require too much money or effort to either bring home or raise. While the latter may be true, the former statement may depend on your purpose behind bringing home Quail. In theory, any pet or domesticated animal, let alone a Quail, can make a considerable dent in your monthly savings, by way of upkeep and maintenance. The advantage of raising Quail over other animals and even poultry, however, is that they can quickly and easily turn into a profitable venture for you, making every penny worth the investment.

As a potential caregiver, you will first need to invest approximately USD 500 to 1000 (around 300 to 700 British pounds) to create a set-up for your Quail. Depending on the number of Quail you plan to bring home, an average-sized cage with no extra attachments will cost you between 250 and 500 USD (150-300 British pounds).

This price excludes the inner elements that make up an ideal environment for your pair or flock. You will have to provide furnishings and flooring elements, such as wood shavings, chippings and bark pieces, and invest in materials that help create hiding and nesting zones. This phase of preparing the habitat should set you back by around 200 USD (125 British pounds), but can also amount to a larger sum, depending on the number of elements and quality of components you add to the environment.

The next financial considerations should be made towards the food you provide your birds with. Your Quail, especially if brought home as babies, will need a steady diet of starter feed and supplements. As they grow, you can monitor their feeding habits and adjust their feed based on their purpose as adult Quail. To start, stocking up on food for your pets will cost you at least 50 USD (30 British pounds), and will then most likely rise based on the size of your flock.

You may find that you can cut down on some expenses in the housing phase by using old containers for nesting, vessels for feeding, and construction materials from around your premises. When it comes to the feed and medical supplies, however, avoid finding cheaper alternatives and select only the best options for your Quail.

None of the above expenses even begin to cover the healthcare your Quail will require, from regular monthly check-ups to a probable antibiotic procedure or two. It is only once these primary arrangements are made that you can consider the cost of the Quail themselves.

The average cost of purchasing a Quail ranges from 3 to 20 USD (1 to 12 British pounds), depending on the source your bird is acquired from. Private breeders and fanciers are known for raising Coturnix and Bobwhite with calmer dispositions and more vibrant coloring than their store-bought counterparts - but they also cost more than the latter.

Many varieties of quail are sold by breeders and fanciers who offer to ship the pets to locations that allow the ownership of the animals. Since the United Kingdom is a popular source of reputed Quail breeders, your shipping fees may add up to 200 USD (120 British pounds), or even higher.

For a healthy quality of life that is neither too sparse nor too excessive for the birds, you should be prepared to part with about 750 USD (500 British pounds) as an initial investment, and then budget around 100 USD (75 British pounds) every month for habitat upkeep, food and healthcare.

2.   Bringing home a Male or Female Quail – and at what age

When you decide to bring home a Quail, you should also take the time to consider the preferred age of your soon-to-be family members. Many potential Quail owners often find themselves conflicted between the choice to bring home fully-grown adult Quails or raise baby hatchlings into adults. Your ultimate decision should be one that addresses the purposes behind bring home Quail.

The first issue that you should address is the purpose of the new Quail in your household - are they your first Quail, or are they brought to add to an already existing flock? If this is your first experience with handling and caring for Quail, it may be preferable to bring adult birds, and care for the young when subsequent eggs are laid.

This does not mean that young Quail should not be considered at the time of purchase - simply that they require more exacting care than their adult counterparts. If you can raise hatchlings in a stable and calm environment, you can also control how temperamental or sociable your Quail will grow up to be. Quail hatchlings also tend to be friendlier and more approachable towards other animals than their adult counterparts, and so make a healthy addition to a mixed-animal setting, even if they have to be housed separately.

Perhaps the biggest advantage, however, that comes with bringing home a Quail hatchling is their hygienic and healthy condition. Young hatchlings are less likely to have transmitted infectious bacteria, and you can ensure that they are raised in the best conditions.

If you already have your own community of Quail at home, however, hatchlings may not easily blend into an already evolved environment. An adult community of Quail requires an adult Quail to properly adapt to the generally aggressive initiation ritual that is establishing a new pecking order. While your society of Quail may shun and even bully younger hatchlings, they are more likely to treat an adult Quail with acceptance.

The true advantage in bringing home an adult Quail lies in the productive value they can have for you. Based on your needs, you can bring home an adult female Quail to supply eggs for hatching or consumption. If a thriving and productive Quail community is your goal, you can bring home a flock comprising one cockerel and some female Quail, without having to wait for them to pass their formative years. Many Quail breeders and hobbyists also like to bring home rare species of adult Quails for exhibition purposes.

Should you choose to house adults together for the purposes of breeding, the optimum ratio for such breeds as the Coturnix varieties are one cockerel for every three to four hens. A higher or lower rate of cockerels in the flock may lead to aggressive interactions preceding the mating ritual, even resulting in cannibalistic fights to the death. If you choose to purchase such breeds as Button Quail or Bobwhite, however, it may be wiser to bring home a pair of adults instead of a flock, owing to their preference for monogamy.

No matter what the age of the Quail you ultimately do bring home, it is essential that the animal be in as healthy a state as possible. Have your Quail checked for any existing medical conditions, and give an initial period in quarantine, till they adapt to their surroundings.

3. Legal Considerations

For those who like the husbandry perspective on domestication that Quail offer, the birds make for rewarding companions. If you choose to acquire Quail, it becomes necessary to take a special interest in the process through which your pet reaches you. Vast though their natural range may be, not all Quail can be picked from the wild and raised at the individual's will. Those potential pet owners living in the United Kingdom have little cause for concern regarding the legality of owning a Coturnix Quail. Sourced from around the continent, Japan and China, several coturnix and some Colinus Quail can be purchased from any reputed pet store dealing in poultry. In recent times, some varieties of Bobwhite and Californian Quail from the North American continent have made their way to the United Kingdom, and can also be acquired with relative ease. For potential pet owners in the United States, however, the ownership of Quail poses certain legal obstacles.

The withdrawing nature of some New World breeds, aversion to domestication and relative scarcity in numbers means that several New World Quail breeds receive special protection from many states across the North American continent. Some of these rules lay restrictions on the possession of certain breeds; other laws may prohibit the acquisition or ownership of a certain breed altogether. In order to protect yourself, is it essential that you understand which members of the Quail family are available for a domestic livelihood in your area.

As a potential poultry farmer, the United States and United Kingdom, among other countries also require you to register your poultry with the Husbandry and Poultry Services; this measure helps the relevant authorities keep the spread of avian diseases and infections in check. If you are already raising other poultry or livestock, you require special permits and need to meet certain prerequisites in order to raise your birds.

Hunting or rearing such breeds as the Montezuma Quail for their meat is illegal in most parts of the United States. You may want to divert your attention to other varieties, such as the Bobwhite family, or one of the Coturnix breeds; be warned, however, that even these options may not be a possibility without necessary certification in some states.

The question then arises, "can I legally own a Quail at all in the United States or United Kingdom?" If you wish to bring home a single Quail or a pair, such breeds as the Button and some Coturnix varieties can be acquired without much legal hassle. To be sure, however, a quick perusal of the local Wildlife laws that govern each territory reveals that authorities mostly work to protect those species of Quail that are native to their land. It is generally only these breeds that will have specific guidelines dictating the terms of their sale, acquisition or ownership. As a rule of thumb, is best to consider Coturnix Quail as pets in those states that may be excessively protective of their indigenous animals.

Therefore, while you still may not be able to either bring home certain varieties of Quail, you most certainly can give a safe and happy home to one of the many healthy Coturnix, Button or Bobwhite varieties available for sale.

If you aren't sure whom to ask for the right legal information concerning the acquisition and ownership of Quail as pets, you can find plenty of literature on this subject on the Internet. Each state's government website details information on the purchase and possession of flora and fauna. Browse through the Game and Wildlife pages for the most accurate and up-to-date information.

4.   Pros and Cons of Quail Ownership

As aviary pets that may not always be social, Quail may not have the universal appeal that dogs and cats command as companionship-worthy species. They demand secure and hygienic housing, diet and health conditions in order to thrive, and take relatively longer to condition than other popular pet species. For the discerning eye that understands the value of the Quail - as an exhibition bird, a melodious companion or as a producer of viable meat and eggs, however, raising Quail can turn into a therapeutic and rewarding experience.

Pros of raising Quail

Despite their slightly fussy nature, Quail can be advantageous to their caregivers in the following ways:

● Diurnal by nature, Quail are active by day and asleep during the night hours, making them easy to care for and interact with during the waking hours, if this be your daily routine.

● While in their cage, Quail raised in captivity can be social with their housemates, and are entertaining, both to watch and listen to. They spend their waking hours either engaging in foraging or nesting behaviours, and communicate with each other's through a series of distinct sounds - some of which sounds like short bursts of giggling.

● Quail are among the cleanest of the poultry species, and engage in dust bathing behaviours to rid their plumage of mites and parasites. They may require little or no intensive grooming on your part, aside from the occasional wash if you bring home an exhibition Quail species.

● Some breeds of Quail, particularly the Coturnix varieties, also possess a fairly high level of emotional intelligence, and can be trained to respond to certain sounds and calls, along with basic commands as fetching and retrieval.

● Quail are hardy and robust little creatures, with immune systems that can resist most infections - health problems, if any, will often result from infections sustained in an unhygienic housing environment, a deficit in nutritional requirements, or wounds and injuries sustained due to fighting.

Cons of raising Quail

Among those who have not raised a Quail, or any type of poultry before, it is a common misconception that small to medium-sized birds such as chickens and Quail require as little care as a canary or parrot kept in the cage. This harbored notion, however, could not be further from the truth.

As is common with all poultry raised either for personal use or for profit, Quail, too, require a sizeable initial investment and sustained maintenance costs in order to be viable to you. They are less likely to adapt their lifestyle and dietary requirements to suit yours; rather it is you whose schedule will have to complement the Quail's daily needs in order for it to survive. As personable and low-maintenance as they can be in the home of the right owner in the long-term, here are some of the ways through which Quail could become a disadvantage to unprepared or unwilling owners:

● Quail can be very needy as pets. Apart from timely feeding and health check-ups, you will also have to spend at least an hour playing with the pet each day, as prolonged distance from the owner may cause the rodent to revert back to its wild state.

● They demand a lot of attention from caregivers, especially as babies. The amount of time you spend caring for your Quail affects how early and how firmly the pet will bond with you.

● Some breeds of New World quail, particularly bobwhites or Button Quail, either cannot be handled for long periods of time, or, prefer to be touched or held only when they please. Despite plenty of attention and devoted towards your birds, the Quail may also spend the entirety of their stay with you trying to escape from their housing.

● Personality-wise, Quail can either be shy and withdrawing or even aggressive and hostile, depending on the breed. Pet owners often narrate tales of the Quail regularly displaying varying degrees of dominance and aggression towards other mates or the caregiver themselves, based on their individual personalities.

● Quail are known to nip or attack other cage mates, or even their caregiver. It must be noted, however, that Quail will seldom bite without reason - if they do, it is most often an instinctual response to be held or touched.

• If you are looking for a quiet pet who keeps to themselves, do not be fooled by the Quail's cute appearance and small size. Mischievous by nature, they can be relatively destructive when let outside the cage. They are also prone to predator attacks, and will need costly security measures to feel secure.

• Even though there are plenty of success stories among people who have raised Quail, owing to the individualistic personality of the bird, they may never completely become friendly towards you, despite your best efforts.

Chapter 4: Selecting your Quail

Once you have put careful thought into the consequences that bringing home a Quail can have, it is best to find the right sources to purchase your Quail from. Buying a Quail takes more effort than walking into a shop and selecting the prettiest bird; a variety of factors determine whether the Quail on offer is in good enough condition to take home with you. When you set out to buy a Quail, aim to return with the healthiest bird of the bunch. You can only receive a complete bill of health from your local poultry expert, but a few simple physical indicators should reveal the state of health of your prospective Quail:

1. The eyes of the Quail should be clear, and not clouded over, sunken or oozing any liquids,
2. A healthy Quail hatchling can walk almost immediately after they hatch. Any hatchling that is lethargic or immobile is unhealthy,
3. The Quail should either be flapping its wings or have them resting flatly against its body. Any irregular positioning of the wing signals injury, even deformity,
4. The plumage and coat should cover the body entirely; patchy coats or missing feathers hint at an aggressive, even sick bird.
5. Healthy Quail will be active; either exploring the house or scurrying into hiding spaces, even in a closed setting,
6. A healthy Quail will constantly look for food sources; lack of appetite is an indicator of poor health,
7. While Quail are messy, they are not unhygienic. If the prospective Quail is covered in his own fecal matter, which is alarmingly smelly, or is covered in mites and is not dust-bathing, the Quail is not healthy.
8. Ensure that the nose is not runny or swollen, as this may indicate an infection that the Quail will carry for life and possibly spread to other birds.

9. Finally, check the Quail for visible injuries, scars, sores or wounds. Only if the Quail can clear all your health inspection should you ask the vendors for the price.

1.   Best Quail breeds to bring home

Based on your geographical location, your level of expertise at raising any type of poultry, and more importantly, your purpose of bringing home a Quail, there are a host of breeds for you to pick from. Each breed brings with it a unique set of physical characteristics, demeanor, and social habits. You may find that some birds are more high-maintenance in terms of care and handling than others. While some varieties possess a striking appearance that distinguishes them from their cousins.

Ultimately, the breeds you do purchase will have to be best-suited to your needs and preferences as a Quail owner. If you plan to make a living out of rearing your Quail, there are several varieties that have been bred to produce either a higher quantity of eggs per year or supply a superior quality of meat. There are also those breeds whose meat and eggs are of equal value in the market. Still other varieties are bred and raised for decorative and exhibitory purposes only - of striking plumage and exotic demeanor, these varieties are generally only raised by professional Quail farmers.

With time, practice and a hands-on experience with your Quail, you will better learn which breeds are the right ones for your house or farm. Until you achieve that level of expertise, here are a few suggestions to help make your purchase easier:

- For a bird that is easy to raise, has a pleasant demeanor, produces a high number of eggs and good quality meat, opt for the Coturnix family of quail.
- Quail from the Coturnix family, such as Jumbo, Texas A&M and English White have all been bred for their meat-production value; any of these varieties are ideal for those Quail raised for meat.
- If you plan on raising Quail for the purpose of egg-production and consumption, whether for personal or

commercial use, pick the Coturnix quail for an easy option, or try the Bobwhite Quail if you can handle mildly temperamental birds as an amateur poultry owner.

- Bobwhites, along with Gambel's and Mountain Quail, make excellent pets for those who want to raise Quail as exhibition or decorative birds. Their vibrant plumage and majestic appearance makes them an ideal entrant at several poultry competitions.
- If you seek personal companionship from a pair of Quail, and can handle the rare small and abrupt burst of aggression, Button Quail are both a pleasing as well as beautiful breed to bring home.
- For those Quail owners who have the access and legal permission, as well as the commitment required to raise this bird, a rare species such as the Montezuma Quail would make an ideal and quirky pet. Depending on the laws governing your area, you may require licenses to own and house the pet, or may only be able to acquire eggs instead of bringing home a bird from the wild. This breed is usually reserved only for the experienced poultry owner.

2.   The price of Quail

How much you pay to bring home your Quail will vary on a number of deciding factors - the source that you buy the Quail from, the number of Quail you decide to buy, the age of the Quail at the time of purchase, their physical appearance and plumage, and the breed itself, just to name a few. Furthermore, an always-fluctuating market for the purchase of poultry makes it difficult to pin down a uniform price on the Quail of your choice.

Despite minor differences in the prices, you will generally be able to acquire Quail hatchlings with common Coturnix and Colinus varieties selling for anywhere between £1 to £4 (1.5 - 5 USD) per adult cockerel, and £3 to £12 (4.5 - 18 USD) per Quail hen. Hatchlings will cost you less, especially if bought in a large group, but the prices for those breeds with rare color coats and superior lineage may set you back by up to 20 to 30 per Quail. Do not be too surprised if your vendor or breeder quotes an unreasonable amount for a rare breed Quail such as the Montezuma in their shops - decorative prized birds commands sums of money that often run upwards of hundreds of dollars or pounds!

3.   Buying from Breeders

When you begin your research to find reliable sources to purchase Quail, most suggestions will point you towards Quail breeders, and with good reason. Breeders are among the most passionate and enthusiastic caregivers you will find, and always raise high-quality Quail for sale.

Since this is a means of earning and way of life for them, Quail breeders will have eggs, hatchlings and adults Quail for sale all year round. You will also have the opportunity to better study the difference between different broiler and layer breeds, and may even spot such poultry as chickens, pheasant, Quail and turkeys for sale, as breeders often raise more than three or four species at a time.

Quail breeders are very particular about such factors as the health of the Quail, the housing and safety conditions provided to the flock, the quality of their feed, their physical appearance and their overall temperament. Unlike many retail vendors, Quail breeders raise their birds themselves, have extensive knowledge of the breed and even lineage of the birds, and can confidently guarantee you a Quail of both high breeding and good health.

Breeders are often the best people to contact when you need assistance in matters such as finding a poultry expert, receiving the right permits for registration and sale of produce, etc. Furthermore, breeders seldom charge exorbitant prices for their birds; most are happy to offer them at very reasonable rates. Should you find a suitable breeder in your area, try to forge a relationship with them. They may turn out to be your greatest allies in your endeavor to raise Quail.

4. Buying from Vendors

When you think of buying a new Quail, your most obvious option may be the local pet retail store. It should be noted, however, that not all retail vendors will stock up on the breed of Quail you may be looking for, and may not be able to guarantee you a bird in the pink of health.

Quail require extremely clean surroundings, fresh feed and an attention to their comfort and well-being that the vendors may not be able to provide. You may find the Japanese Coturnix and Bobwhite Quail with relative ease, but other breeds such as the Chinese Button Quail, the California Quail and Gambel's Quail may be trickier to track down with all local vendors.

When you do find a suitable and reputed Quail vendor, however, you give yourself a number of buying advantages. Vendors, if knowledgeable in their trade, can offer you a variety of Quail based on your need, from broiler breeds to layer breeds, all with differently colored plumage. This gives you the freedom to select a Quail after evaluating all your options.

An experienced Quail vendor is also a reliable source for any information that you may need for your Quail's welfare. They will usually have reliable poultry experts to recommend, and can also guide you towards finding the right housing and feeding supplies for your Quail. The more professional of these vendors also offer basic health benefits and care packages for your flock, so do enquire about these facilities.

You should bear in mind that such professional services will cost some money, definitely more than a breeder would charge you. Professional vendors, however, will not overcharge you for your birds, especially if you are buying them in a group. The price may be only reasonably higher than that of the breeder, but will ensure a trusted source for your purchase.

5.   Acquiring from Individuals

While this may be the most uncommon of all your buying choices, Quail hobbyists and owners will also give up hatchlings and even adults for sale. Some Quail owners often find themselves with more hatchlings than they can take care of, owing to constraints in budget or space, or the prolific egg-laying abilities of our female friends. If the number is too large for them to raise on their own, you will find advertisements posted by Quail pet owners on such public forums as newspapers, community message boards and online service websites.

Buying your Quail from enthusiasts and owners can often be your best choice, if you are able to track down such sellers. Experienced Quail owners raise their animals in optimum conditions, provide individual attention towards the bird's health, and will mostly sell you healthy birds at very reasonable rates.

6.   Adopting Quail

In case you don't want to spend lots of money to purchase a Quail, or cannot find a trusted source in your area to buy one from, you can choose to adopt a Quail from a shelter closest to you.

Adoption is often a rewarding experience for the bird keeper, as well as the Quail itself. By making this choice, you can bring home and nurture a pet of your own. Adopting a Quail, in addition, can also benefit your health by adding nutrition to your table.

When you find a Quail that you'd like to adopt, ensure that you have it examined for any ailments, infections or other health conditions. Even if you do find a perfectly healthy Quail, understand that it will need constant care through food, water and medical attention. The bird may need even more nurturing and behavioral therapy if it has had a traumatic past in the wild or with a previous owner.

The choice to adopt Quail comes with its own set of responsibilities and duties, but if you have the commitment and patience to raise your Quail, adopting your pet will be one of the best decisions you make.

7.   Where to buy Quail in the UK and USA?

Even though Quail may be most easily available through local pet stores, it is advisable to buy such birds as Quail from more reputed sources like breeders. whether you live in the United States or United Kingdom, breeders are often trusted more than any other source to sell potential owners pets who have been tamed and vaccinated.

If you live in the United States, most breeders and fanciers will place advertisements for Quail for sale on such websites as McMurray Hatchery, Gamebird Farm, Purely Poultry and Cyber Quail. In the United Kingdom, Quail for sale can be found on websites as Chickens Allotment Garden, Quail Farm, Quails in Essex, www.birdtrader.co.uk

8.   Initial Checkups and Vaccinations

Regardless of the source through which you purchase your Quail, and robust of health though they may generally be, it is essential that they receive medical attention before they are brought home. Depending on the care provided to your Quail before its sale, you may need to verify that your pet has no underlying illnesses or infections; you may also have to administer a dose of initial vaccinations.

Quail that have been acquired from such reputed as breeders and fanciers are often healthy and have already been given their course of Quail Bronchitis vaccinations - especially if they are Bobwhites. Most Quail, owing to a complex high proportion of the necessary enzymes and hormones, are relatively immune to such infections as the Avian flu, and may not need vaccinations unless they have become a carrier.

In the event that they haven't performed the initial check-up and vaccination procedures, your breeder or fancier will usually inform you in advance. To prevent any chance of bringing home a potential carrier of infections, however, ensure that you ask your breeder or fancier for the necessary health certificates proving that your Quail has been vaccinated and cleared for husbandry purposes.

Other sources such as pet store vendors may or may not have their Quail vaccinated against Bronchitis; the care provided to pets within a store is usually determined by the dedication of the vendor towards selling healthy birds. Quail acquired from pet stores may also have sustained wing injuries or contracted respiratory or parasitic infections from other members in the cage that are not instantly visible. To avoid any such mishaps, it is best to make an appointment with a reputed poultry expert for an initial round of check-ups on the day that your purchase your Quail.

9.   Can Quail be Electronically Tagged?

Ideally, a domesticated pet or animal raised in a nurturing environment should be loyal to its immediate surroundings, and not venture too far from their homes. In the case of such pets as dogs or cats, adequate training and care is usually enough to ensure that the pet does not run away. As birds who spend much of their lifespan in the wild evading capture from predators, however, Quail, though they can be conditioned against flying, cannot always be prevented from escaping their cages and out of the house through an open door or window.

Curious and oftentimes suspicious by nature, even the tamest Quail will usually want to explore its immediate surroundings, and could easily become lost. Devices such as embedded microchips act as tracking equipment to help return lost and found birds to their owners. In addition, the microchips can also record such information as the breed of the animals and the vaccinations provided, helping your veterinarian monitor your pet's care more efficiently.

Electronic tags are most commonly suggested for such animals as dogs, cats, and those domestic animals who have been raised for profit, such as goats and chickens. However, electronic tagging is not restricted to certain species of animals; it is, in fact, recommended among as many domesticated Quail as possible.

Not much larger than a grain of rice, an electronic microchip is available in different models and can easily be inserted by a reputed veterinarian with a simple procedure, should you choose to have your pet electronically tagged. This procedure is also relatively painless, and will hurt your Quail only as much as the prick of a needle would.

Most pet stores and breeders across the United States and United Kingdom choose to have pets such as dogs and cats electronically tagged, but this requirement may vary among Quail breeders and vendors. As with vaccinations, it is best to check with your breeder if your pet has been tagged, as ownership details on the microchip will have to be transferred under your name and address.

Tagging for poultry raised for profit

When you bring home a covey of Quail for the purpose of raising them for their meat and eggs, you may be required by your state or country's Husbandry laws, to add electronic tags for all your poultry. These RFID tags, far from being inserted into the skin of the Quail, are merely clipped on to the foot of the bird with the help of a plastic tag. Embedded with a microchip that identifies and tracks the location of the bird, tagging your poultry has a multitude of benefits for you as a poultry farmer.

Built to fit around your Quail's feet as a day-old chick, the band can also be stretched as the bird grows. Slotted with an identification tag, you now have complete access towards identifying which birds among your flock are prolific layers, which birds are ready for culling, and which members may be victims or carriers of infections. The bands are also available in variations, so they can be attached around the neck, ear or wing, and are available with a barcode option, that ascertains a unique identification to your bird in the poultry market.

If you are required by state laws, or choose to attach identification tags, whether electronic or barcoded, such websites as www.tagfaster.com provide tagging solutions in the United Kingdom, France and Australia. RFID Shop and Ketchum, on the other hand, provide the same services in the United States.

Chapter 5: Housing your Quail

Housing conditions for your Quail should and will be among your chief priorities when you decide to bring them home. Since many Quail species adapt easily to a variety of surroundings, you will have great flexibility when determining the ideal housing space for them.

You may have the resources to provide your Quail with a natural outdoor enclosure, foraging and hiding spots, and maximum security against predators. Or you may prefer that your Quail roam freely in your backyard, enclosed within cages containing little crates of water for feeding.

You may live in a cold area that requires additional heating to keep your Quail warm, or may live in a tropical area that will need cooling facilities. Do not fret over which housing condition is ideal for your Quail; there are plenty of options that come with their own benefits and drawbacks.

Quail owners generally design housing spaces to blend the environmental conditions with the needs of their birds; this is essential for their emotional well-being and egg-productivity. To be at their most comfortable, your Quail require cosy nesting spots, ample food and water sources, space to exercise their feet and perch, and some form of security against possible predators. So long as the above, and the following factors are considered, you can easily modify your surroundings to house your flock:

1. Adequate number of nooks, crannies and personal zones for all your Quail. These spaces are used by the Quail, especially the Bobwhite and Gambel breeds, when they need "alone time" hiding spaces, and are essential to maintain a calm environment.

2. Optimum temperatures within the space that help keep your Quail comfortable. While hatchlings require their heating conditions to be constantly monitored, adult Quail can easily adapt to a predetermined temperature, preferably around 55 degrees Fahrenheit.

3. The degree of security you want to provide to your Quail. Different housing options come with their own sets of drawbacks, especially in terms of protection against predators; Quail require heightened security against predatory animals, more so than other poultry. In addition, the cage itself has to be free of unhygienic conditions or toxic growth.

4. The amount of freedom you want to give your Quail, for exploration as well as possible escape. Certain housing options are more effective than others at preventing your Quail from flying away or escaping. If you have opted against practices such as pinioning and feather clipping, you will have to decide how your housing space may prevent or encourage unwanted escapes.

5. The accessibility of the housing areas to your own is also a crucial factor. While you don't want the Quail to be located too far from your eye, their enclosures - especially for larger flocks - should also not crowd areas like picnic spots or play areas used by your children. The eventual aim of the enclosure is to merge seamlessly into your personal space.

1.   Setting up a House for your Quail

To complement their small sizes, Quail require a small and low-heighted enclosure within which to roam, nest, rest and hide at their convenience. As active and inquisitive birds prone to bursts of aggression towards housemates in cramped quarters, Quail will require a housing area that are not only spacious, but also filled with plenty of hiding spots that provide privacy.

Depending on the extent of your endeavour and your purpose for housing Quail, you can either set up an outdoor housing facility in your backyard or farm, or can also choose to house your birds indoors. The house itself can be a small wire cage, a rabbit hutch, a short bird aviary, or even an aquarium; any housing container that provides at least a foot in length and no more than two feet in height is ideal for an adult Quail. Aviaires are considered popular housing options despite their tall build; should you choose a cage with extra height, create a buffer between the Quails and the hard ceiling by installing a layer of netting. If an aquarium is your preferred housing of choice (also ideal for a pair of Quail), ensure that the tank has a capacity of least 20 gallons.

Ideally, an adult Quail housed in captivity requires a cage that is at least two feet high and three feet long and two feet wide (50 x 150 x 50 cm). Another important factor to consider is the distance provided between cage wiring. A wire distance ranging between 10 and 15 millimetres is needed to help keep your Quail from poking their heads or slipping out, and to help keep other pets, such as dogs and cats, and predators such as raccoons, skunks and foxes from reaching for Quail within. As an added precautionary measure, cage doors should be fitted with latches and barricades that are sturdy enough to withstand manipulation and damage from Quail and other small animals.

Such dimensions also make small bird cages and housing meant for guinea pigs and hamsters a popular choice. Large aviaries, squirrel and chinchilla cages sold at pet stores should have the measurements necessary for your Quail's comfort. Most commercially manufactured cages will either made entirely out of wire, or may be sold in wood-and-wire combination variants. Either of these is suitable for your pets - a wood-bottomed cage with a detachable bottom tray would be ideal. In the event that you find narrow cages with adequate height, two cages can also be combined together to provide more room for a pair or more of Quail.

The cages themselves will have to be housed on a premise that permits Quail to wander outside the cages without fear of injury or attack. Large though they may be, cages are often insufficient in terms of exercise and exploration space needed for the Quail. While Quail enjoy perching atop logs and branches, they will be more prone to taking flight, should they find their housing quarters cramped, hostile or monotonous. If you have decided against clipping the birds' wings, ensure that outdoor housing areas are heavily fenced and provided with a cloth or net ceiling to prevent escape.

Owing to the exacting standard needed to comfortably house a solitary Quail, let alone a group of exotics, finding the ideal cage or enclosure can pose a considerable challenge. Most pet stores stock cages that are wider than they are long, and enclosures for Quail may needed to be ordered in advance. If you find yourself facing a similar challenge, and possess basic carpentry skills, it may be more convenient - and economical - to source the necessary materials and build the cage yourself. Many independent furniture repairs shops and contractors will also build you a cage that suits your requirements for 100-200 USD (65-130 GBP) within a day, if they have the time and materials.

Raising your Quail on the wire
Enclosed cages erected directly on the ground are perfect spaces for your Quail to retreat in; but having a pen share a common flooring with the earth also makes for extra cleaning for you. The main advantage behind having an elevated enclosure is the promise of a cleaner and healthier environment for your Quail.

Any mess in the form of food, water or droppings will slip through the wire flooring and can be cleaned off the ground without disturbing your Quail or coming into direct contact with them. With some simple construction work, you can easily raise the wire cage off the floor. This may take some work and preparation, but will be a convenient option for you in the long term.

A raised cage is nothing but a regular cage that has been erected atop a wooden flooring space, or secured atop a wooden frame to lift the cage off the ground. The wooden flooring for the cage catches the excrement and food particles that slide through the cracks to the ground. The exposed sides of the frame can be covered with protective material such as wire mesh to secure the cage against entry by predators.

As comfortable as elevated enclosures will be, you will need to make them comfortable for the Quail by covering the sides of the pen. These covers will shield your Quail predators, harsh weather conditions, and abrupt changes in their surroundings. You can provide an easy cover for your Quail by mounting your cage against a wall, and covering the other three sides.

If you live in cold areas or places with harsh winter months, an open floor may allow windy drafts to seep through the cracks and chill your Quail. You can avoid this by either placing heating pans on the floor, or placing a layer of covering under the porous floor.

Apart from the convenience it provides, raising Quail on the wire is ultimately attractive because it protects your Quail from predatory attacks. Wild animals and birds of prey are highly unlikely to break into a secure pen, especially one that provides the obstacle of being raised off the ground.

The only other preparation you will need to make before erecting raised pens is acquiring the necessary permits from your local authorities. Some areas, especially urban residential spaces, prefer to be informed when a group of 50 or more birds of any breed are collectively housed in the same area. Once you receive the green signal from the required offices, you can implement - and reap- the long-term benefits of elevated pens.

Outdoor Housing for Quail
Plenty of open space to explore and forage is one of the Quail's prime requisites for ideal housing, and the outdoor option of housing is one that most adheres to your Quail's wishes. This setting may not be easy to come by - you'd require a considerable portion of open land at your disposal, depending on the size of your venture as a Quail farmer. And your outdoor housing environment will need a ceiling of some kind, to prevent escape.

If you do own some land, however, you should certainly consider this housing option.

Allowing your Quail to wander about on open land in their natural range closely imitates their natural settings, making them comfortable. Free space to forage, nest and even socialize greatly contributes towards the general well-being of your Quail.

In order to let your Quail roam about freely, however, you will have to ensure that your land is properly protected against predatory attacks. Depending on the predators in your area, protection can vary from erecting a simple fence around your perimeter, to setting up alarms and traps outside your area.

Your Quail will appreciate an open setting to wander in, but this setting also makes them vulnerable to attacks not only from animals on land, but birds of prey as well. Birds such as hawks and falcons find Quail extremely easy to hunt, but will keep away if the Quail have plenty of hiding spaces and cover, or in the presence of a larger animal to guard the flock, such as a guard dog.

An outdoor enclosure for Quail is not the same as providing a free-range option for the birds; letting your Quail go free-range often results in most birds flying away. You will have to select a large coop for housing, construct a run attached to the cage, or will need to enclose the area within a fenced perimeter and a netted, wood, or cloth ceiling.

You may feel like the outdoor option requires extra work and dedication on your part - this is definitely true. The choice of outdoor housing is usually taken only by those who are dedicated to providing a setting that mirrors the Quail's natural environment.

It takes a great deal of responsibility to make the Quail as comfortable as possible, while protecting them from attacks and providing them with constant food and water sources. You will also have to ensure that the flooring of the housing area is kept as clean and parasite and infection-free as possible.

Furthermore, Quail are curious and even messy creatures, who will leave their mark in your immediate surroundings. It is important that the members of your community are open to having a flock of Quail in their setting. Your birds may wander into someone else's yard, pluck at their plants and flowers, may be hunted by other domestic animals, or may become traumatized at contact with a friendly neighbor.

Many owners who choose the outdoor option may already have favorable conditions on their premises, such as tightly-guarded security measures against predators and invaders, a tranquil setting away from neighbors, or chicken coops that have free space for housing.

Nearly all free-range Quail owners also refrain from such practices as pinioning and feather clipping, out of respect for their animals. Once Quail find that their settings provide them with adequate food, water, security and space to roam, they tend to settle within the area. If you share similar conditions, or can provide a relaxed environment for your Quail, the outdoor method of housing may just be the one for you.

2. Furnishing the housing area

Some Quail housed indoors, especially the New World breeds, are often skittish in unfamiliar surroundings, especially for the first few days in a new owner's house. A cage placed in the corner of the room with one side preferably facing a wall and accessorized with plenty of brush cover provides Quail with a safe and familiar corner to which they can retreat in times of stress or perceived threat.

Once a suitable cage, crate, aviary or hutch is selected, it must be furnished in a way that is as close to the Quail's natural surroundings, while also being functional. Padding the floor about 1-2 feet deep with materials that encourage nesting and provide relief from wire flooring should be your first priority. A layer of bedding also helps the Quail stay warm when the temperatures drop, while providing the housing space with an absorbent layer for food remains and fecal matter. You can either incorporate such elements from nature as grass, pine shavings, even large leafy vegetable patches - refrain, however, from using cedar wood shavings; this has been known to cause some level of toxicity in Quail lungs.

Pet owners also choose to pad the floor of the cage with hay and thick strips of cloth, especially for cages with hard floors. Many pet stores carry commercially prepared pet-bedding with a variety of bases, such as coconut husk or paper, and the appropriate one be used for the flooring.

The next essential element in the Quail's cage is a small space at the corner of the cage reserved for dust-bathing activities. Quail generally use dry elements such as sand or dirt to help clean their coats of mites and lice; in an enclosed environment, you will have to provide the necessary materials for the birds. Place a long yet shallow dish, tray or pan in the corner of the cage and fill it with sand or dirt; alternatively you can place this dish inside a large cardboard box with an opening cut out on one side. This prevents the dirt from messing the contents of the cage. You can refill the contents of this tray as and when needed. Diatomaceous earth is also favored by many Quail owners due to its effect at killing parasites off the birds' back while causing no harm to the birds themselves.

In many cases, several Quail breeds will not be particular about finding a safe space to lay their eggs; they tend to drop their eggs rather haphazardly around the cage. This does not mean that Quail cannot be encouraged to lay their eggs in a safe designated nesting space; this may even be essential to prevents eggs from getting damaged in a crowded cage.

As a simple solution, you can provide plenty of brush cover within the housing areas, and supplement this cover with hay bundles. Nest boxes with a small hole for entry and exit are sold for aviary purposes in pet stores, and make for ideal nesting spaces for Quail. The inside of the nest boxes should be lined with soft materials such as hay or strips of cloth that help keep the eggs safe and incubated till you collect them.

If you are raising your Quail on wire, depending on the model and make of your cage, you may need to provide a separate tray under the cage floor to collect droppings, discarded food and stray flooring bits that fall from the cage. Most wire cages have no firm flooring, and can be placed atop a tray or sheets of newspapers, which are collected and cleaned on a daily or weekly basis. If you find cages with detachable cleaning trays, however, extra collection material may not be required.

After the basics of the cage are taken care of, other elements within the cage should all be aimed towards providing comfort and security, as well as ensuring that the Quail does not become bored. Filling their waking hours with such activities as perching, foraging for food around the flooring, nesting and running, with the right accessories in the cage will promote emotional wellbeing and keep behavioral disorders such as feather pecking each other at bay.

There is no limit - or budget - for the amount of accessories that can be added to your cage; on the other hand, Quail are easily pleased and do not require costly furnishings and accessories. At higher points, perches such as small logs for Quail to rest and survey their housing areas on. Small log pieces from fruit trees are safe enough for Quail to perch from, and also emulate the feeling of a natural environment.

At floor level, Quail are perfectly content if provided with brush cover areas and a space for dirt-bathing. Additionally, a basic artificially-constructed network of tunnels and burrows will not only provide safety against predators, but will also encourage nesting habits. These tunnels can easily be crafted using sheets of cardboard and PVC glue. Cardboard sheets are just as useful for constructing nest boxes in corners of the cage for privacy and mating. Large, smooth pebbles and rocks are can also be assembled in small formation around the cage and covered with ample grassy cover - Quail tend to use such spots as hideaways in times of threat.

Housing your Quail indoors

Outdoor housing for your Quail may make your flock more susceptible to attacks from predators or escape, but at least provide the birds with a space to wander and forage. An indoor setting, on the other hand, limits the amount of activity a Quail might receive; your birds will not want to restrict their movements to the confines of the cage or aquarium. They are most content when allowed to explore the entirety of their surroundings - even the room outside their cage. Promoting free-range roaming is also a healthy habit that instills a sense of security in your flock, and helps New World breeds bond faster with their caregivers. Several elements in a human habitat, however, may either harm delicately-built creatures like Quails, or they, in turn, may gnaw on prized possessions in the house.

It is a combination of the need for ample space for cages and exploring that makes empty, undisturbed rooms in the house a perfect spot to house Quail in. Such objects as electrical fittings and sharp furniture should be moved out of the room, along with other destructible items placed at floor level. Windows in the room should ideally be locked firmly to prevent Quail from escaping out of the room. If threatened in a new environment, Quail will also try to fly upward; to prevent "head-boink" incidents, ensure that ceiling fans are switched off, fancy lighting fixtures are dismantled and cleared away, and that there are no sharp hooks or edges jutting out from the roof of the room.

Quail have an inherently inquisitive nature, and many breeds, particularly Button Quail, like to explore their surroundings by tasting items they find curious. If the space outside their cage must be reserved for wandering, ensure that all hazardous objects, such as sharp items, small toys that may choke the Quail and potentially toxic food, vegetation, insect sprays and chalk are kept away from the room. Do not let your Quail venture into such areas as the bathroom or the kitchen; a heated stovetop or open toilet bowl may cause unnecessary harm to your bird. Quail are also often at risk of being stepped on by members in the house as they hurry across the floor; they are just as likely to be chased or even eaten by larger pets on the premises. To prevent such accidents, it is best to keep the room locked at all times, save for feeding, cleaning and egg-collecting sessions.

Rooms meant for Quail housing can also serve as storage areas for their personal belongings. Several Quail owners use an empty tool shed, garage or even the attic in their houses as a safe housing and storage area. Chests filled with feeding, cleaning and medical supplies for the housing zone can be installed in this room (provided they are locked securely), to help contain all Quail-related activity within the area.

3.   Maintaining a Hygienic Housing Environment

You may spend large sums of money to provide the best housing conditions for your Quail, but if you cannot provide the time and commitment required to clean and maintain the environment, you expose your flock to a variety of possible infections, ailments and emotional distress. Proper hygiene can be maintained within the cage in the following ways:

1. A regular inspection and cleaning of the pens is essential; Quail will deposit fecal matter, discarded food particles and eggs on the flooring on a daily basis.
2. The feeding bowls and water-feeders should be cleaned once or twice a week, and water-feeders in particular, should be disinfected once a month.
3. The Quail should be placed in a separate cage or shifted to another premises till the cleaning and disinfecting process is complete, in order to prevent them from contracting allergies or infections from old particles.
4. Existing pens should be wiped clean, emptied of old flooring and bedding layers, and then be sterilized with the help of a poultry-safe disinfectant.

5. Before you transfer the Quail back into the cage, replace all old bedding with fresh materials. The floor bedding will have to be changed every two to three weeks. This is important as the old bedding will, at one point, have no more room for moisture absorption. It will also have become too dirty from collection of fecal matter and cannot be kept in the cage without the risk of contaminating the environment.

6. A good way of telling that it is time to change your substrate is when the flooring begins emitting a faint yet rank odor. If left unattended, this damp smell may become more intense, signalling the rotting and decomposing of your substrate.

Chapter 6: Feeding your Pet Quail

1.   What to feed your Quail

You may have fed slices of bread to the Quail at a public park; but understand that your Quail cannot live on scraps alone. Just as you would put effort into feeding your dog or cat specific types of food, the food that Quail receive requires equal thought.

To make matters convenient for you and your Quail, you can choose to provide feed that is manufactured to suit their health requirements. While this form of diet is sufficient for your Quail's well-being, you can also encourage them to find their own food by foraging in their surrounding areas.

1. Natural Forage

Essentially, Quail can survive perfectly well on the commercially prepared food that you provide; in fact, this feed has been formulated keeping the dietary requirements of your birds in mind. Natural forage or fresh produce is usually only added to the Quail's diet as a supplement.

In theory, Quail should be able to forage for their own food among the flowers, shrubs, worms and small insects available in their vicinity. As poultry is raised either for meat or eggs, however, a regulated commercially-manufactured feed best ensures that the birds receive most or all of their nutritional intake; this reduces the effort of you having to produce natural sources of food on a daily basis. In addition, the excess nutrients provided by foods accepted by Quail, such as grains or legumes, may upset the nutritional equilibrium created by commercially manufactured feed.

This does not mean that you eliminate all natural food from the bird's' diet. Fond of such foods as legumes, grains, grain products such pasta, corn, apples and lettuce, your Quail will be delighted to receive the occasional handful of broken pasta or fruit fed by hand, or added to their feed.

Quail also enjoy the taste of grass and can be fed small handfuls of the same, provided they are clean of any pesticides or chemicals. As omnivores, the birds will also enjoy a mealworm or two fed to them a couple times a week. Encouraging your Quail to feed on natural forage such as flies, mosquitoes, spiders and worms in their vicinity is an economical way to provide nutrition and control the spread of pests in your area.

Not all plants, grasses, fruits and vegetables are safe for a Quail to consume; several plants and foods can cause toxicity, forcing you to restrict their access to vegetation that is compatible with their system. So long as you can exercise some control over the natural food sources available to your flock, natural forage can be an excellent supplement to the Quail's diet and well-being.

2. Commercially Prepared Foods
As beneficial as natural foraging may be for your well-being of your Quail, in a domestic setting, it works best only as a supplement to your Quail's diet. Your own settings may not have adequate foraging sources, and the Quail' curious natures may prompt them to wander too far from your premises.

You will still need to be the primary provider of food for your flock. By supplying your Quail with the right amount of food at scheduled times, you can prevent them from relying too heavily on natural forage. Your most reliable feeding options for this purpose are commercially manufactured foods prepared especially for the Quail.

Besides containing carefully calculated quantities of your Quail's daily nutritional requirement, commercially-manufactured feed also helps rear your Quail to your suiting, if you are breeding them for husbandry purposes. Quail require different forms of nutrition depending on their age, gender and role in animal husbandry.

If you have to feed hatchlings and younger members, you have to include significant amounts of tissue-building protein. Protein is especially important if you are raising Quail for their eggs. Ideally, protein forms about 24-28 percent of a growing Quail's diet, which can be provided through special "starter-feed" packs.

As the Quail age and progress past six weeks for a Coturnix and eight weeks for a Bobwhite, they can progress to foods that substitute excess protein for other essential nutrients. A common mistake that amateur Quail owners make is to assume that the feed manufactures for a certain bird is suitable to all birds in general. When selecting feed for your Quail, ensure that it has been prepared for the type of bird you wish to raise - "developer feed" for layer breeds raised to produce high number of eggs, and "finisher feed: for broiler breeds raised to provide meat for consumption.

Chicken feed in particular, is usually boosted with a nutritional content that is complementary to the dietary needs of Quail and can be provided if Quail feed is hard to come by. If all else fails, you can always contact your Quail seller, fowl expert or breeder for advice. These are people who are invested in the health and welfare of Quail, and can correctly guide you towards finding the right feed in your area or preparing your own.

3. The role of Grit in Quail feed
Quail - like some other birds - digest their food with the help of an organ called the ventriculus, or the gizzard. This organ, however, requires further assistance to help break down bigger particles of food. Sand, tiny particles of dirt and other such grainy objects collected by the Quail while foraging make for perfect teeth-like substitutes for Quail.

Quail who forage in the wild can collect their own sand or grainy dirt - commonly known as grit. When you are the sole provider of food for your Quail, however, they have no means of finding sufficient grit for their gizzards.

You may not notice it immediately, but the amount of grit a Quail consumes greatly affects the performance of their gizzards. The more grainy substances the Quail have to break down harder food, the more efficient their gizzards become. The organs also tend to increase in size with additional exercise, helping to build a healthy and strong digestive system in your Quail.

To ensure that your Quail can consume a variety of foods with relative ease, provide them with a steady supply of grit within easy access. If your Quail are allowed to roam outdoors, you do not have to worry about providing any grit for them. If they have been housed indoors, it becomes your responsibility to tend to their needs.

You do not have to fret about mixing your own grit, or determining what materials are safe for your Quail to consume. Nearly all vendors that supply Quail feed also store especially-manufactured bags of grit for your Quail. You can simply place a separate bowl of grit near the feeding containers and let your Quail collect the materials as they require.

Ensure that you do not mix the grit directly with their food; Quail consume grit at different times than food and mixing them together might cause your Quail to swallow the dirt instead of storing it in its gizzard.

4. The need for Oyster Shells in Quail feed

Calcium is a vital mineral for any growing animal as it helps to build and fortify bone structure. Quail, too require significant amounts of calcium during their developing years. Quail hens, in particular, demand a specific and significantly higher supply of calcium for better egg-laying once they reach maturation.

The tricky feature of calcium, however, is that its intake needs to be carefully monitored and regulated. A deficiency of calcium in the feed will result in brittle eggs and weaker bone structure among your females. Eggs that are laid may not hatch if the hen's feed has witnessed a deficiency in calcium content An excess amount of calcium, on the other hand, is just as harmful.

Adult Quail raised as broiler breeds and are not laying eggs will need far less calcium that their egg-laying community members. You will, therefore, have to be alert towards the amount of calcium each member of your flock receives.

Those members that do not need large amounts of calcium will find an adequate supply of the mineral in commercially manufactured feed. You will, however, need to pay close attention to the calcium intake of your female layer breeds.

A potent source of calcium preferred by many Quail breeders is oyster shell, crushed into tiny pieces. The oyster shell can either be sprinkled on the feed of your layer breeds (provided they are housed separately), or even placed separately in a bowl, so your Quail can consume them as per their needs.

If you cannot find oyster shell, you can also use crickets or cuttlebone, rich and common sources of calcium. Cuttlebone and crickets will require some preparation through careful grinding and crushing, but will make for a perfect calcium supplement.

Since calcium is an essential yet tricky mineral to navigate around, any doubts that you may have regarding its intake should be addressed with your waterfowl expert. They will be able to correctly guide you and prevent any calcium-related mishaps from occurring within your flock.

2.   Checklist of food items for your Quail

Fruits	Vegetables	Nuts, seeds, legumes	Grasses, shrubs, plants	Other live feed
Blackberries	Collard greens	Wheat	Dandelion	Crickets
Blueberries	Romaine lettuce	Barley	Clover	Mealworms
Loganberries	Radicchio	Cracked corn	Bermudagrass	Superworms
Cranberries	Carrots	Popcorn	Winter rye grass	Waxworms
Boysenberries	Broccoli	Oats	Fescue grass	Silkworms
Pears	Cabbage	Rice	Zoysia grass	Earthworms
Squash	Cauliflower	Millet	Blue grass	Nightcrawlers
Pumpkin	Asparagus	Peas	Centipedegrass	Red wigglers

Apple	Kale		Rye grass	Moths
Papaya	Beets		Kikuyu grass	
Grapes	Sprouts		Blue grama grass	
Pineapple			Dallis grass	
Watermelon			Wintergrass	
Eggplant			Wheatgrass	
Peaches				
Cucumber				
Figs				
Cantaloupe				
Persimmon				

3.   Frequency

Quail have healthy appetites for their size and need to be supplied with a constant source of food. A balanced diet for your Quail should comprise of a healthy mix of commercially-manufactured feed, along with other nutritional supplements that you may have to provide. Apart from the content of the feed, however, the frequency of food supply is crucial to the well-being and productivity of your Quail.

Adult Quail, whether Coturnix and Bobwhite, require between 17 and 20 grams of feed per day. While you may be able to ascertain the exact feeding times of your birds through observation, most Quail prefer to forage about for their food at their own convenience. Therefore, the smartest way of feeding your Quail may be to simply scatter the feed on the flooring of their pens, or place food bowls or troughs for the birds to feed from.

Feeding bowls are often considered the most convenient way to ensure that the supply of food to the birds is constant, and does not become contaminated through contact with the floor. These bowls or troughs should ideally be placed in a corner of the pen to prevent food particles from spreading across the floor.

Housing pens that have round-the-clock feeding zones, however, generally tend to become messier at a faster rate. You will have to maintain hygienic standards by cleaning out the food trays at least once every two or three days. Inevitable droppings that will collect around nearby areas will also need to be cleared to prevent infections from entering the housing zone. You also have to ensure that your Quail feed is supplemented with plenty of clean water; water trays should be refreshed on a daily basis and can be supplemented with a tablespoon of Apple Cider Vinegar as a supplementary health precaution.

4.   The Importance of Freshness

One factor that ensures the health and wellbeing of your flock and cannot be compromised is the freshness of your feed. Old or stale feed is susceptible to fungal growth and mould that may make your Quail very ill. Furthermore, mould can grow on just about any type of food - from the fresh produce you set aside as food treats to commercially-bought food packages.

The best way to ensure fresh feed for Quail is to find a trusted brand sold by reliable outlets and vendors, and stick with them. Before every purchase, take the time to check if the bags are sealed and the food has been recently manufactured. If you find that the feed is on sale and the price has been steeply reduced, pay close attention to the expiry date and contents. Some vendors may try to lure customers into buying older stock at lower prices to clear their shelves faster.

You may also be attracted to larger bags of feed that are economical provide greater "value for money". Before you make your purchase, understand that the feed catches mould incredibly early once it has been opened. Larger bags of food are a smart choice if you have a big flock, but may not be best for a pair or small group of Quail.

Optimum storage conditions also help to keep your feed fresh for longer. The bag itself may be a good short-term storage option, but if the feed will last you a long time, transfer the contents into airtight containers, preferably marked with the expiry dates.

Every few weeks, take an inventory of the feed you have stored aside. If expired food is harmful to your health, it is equally bad for your Quail. Do not feed them any food that has spoiled, collected mould or its past its shelf-life; any interaction with toxic substances can be fatal to their life.

5.   What not to feed your Quail

Once you settle into a feeding pattern with your Quail, you may find that their palates are surprisingly easy to please; all they require is a constant supply of commercially-manufactured feed to keep them satiated, while the occasional apple slice or lettuce leaf will bring them delight. Such a laidback demeanor may cause some to believe that Quail can be fed almost any type of food; this, however, is far from the truth. If you want to avoid health hazards among your flock, ensure that your Quail stay away from the following foods:

1. Bread is not only a source of minimal nutrition to us, but also to Quail. Composed mainly of empty calories and sugar, Quail have a weakness for bread, and will ignore any nutritious food in its presence. Copious amounts of

bread will fatten up your Quail without providing them with any useful nutrition. In their excitement, your Quail may also try to swallow too much dry bread, which could lead to choking.

2. Certain fruits may be too acidic for your Quail, and cause digestive issues. Citric fruits such as oranges, lemons, and grapefruit are best not fed to your Quail.
3. Other fresh produce that may be healthy for you but is incredibly toxic for Quail includes avocados, onions, shallots and chives. These foods can cause a variety of ailments, ranging from digestive problems and cardiac ailments.
4. Chocolate is also known to be highly toxic for Quail and can lead to poisoning, convulsions, nervous disorders, and death.
5. Processed foods that are high in salts, sugar and unhealthy fats are just as bad for your Quail as they are for you. While they may not be toxic for the Quail, even tiny portions of processed foods may be too fatty for them.
6. Fatty foods in general are best kept away from your Quail along with avocados and fatty processed foods, nuts should also be avoided. Along with filling your Quail with fatty content they don't require, nuts also may become trapped in the Quail's bills and choke them.

6.   Toxicity through Flora and Feed

While we can have considerable information on the health effects that basic fruits and vegetables have on Quail health, we still haven't completely understood which plants bring about toxic reactions in the birds. Based on their ability to adapt to almost any type of environment, it is generally believed that Quail are immune to the toxicity in several if not all plants. Breeders, naturalists, behaviorists and other experts are still trying to ascertain whether this immunity to toxic plants is a physical ability or an instinctual one.

Therefore, while your Quail may not be able to reveal toxic vegetation in your area, you should take the time to inspect the plant life that your Quails will be housed in. Even if the Quail themselves avoid being poisoned, you could easily come into contact with these plants while handling your Quails.

You can also speak to the local flora and fowl experts to discover what local plants may be harmful to your Quail, if any. Familiarize yourself with common plant-life in your region to help avoid any mishaps among your flock.

Toxicity may also be caused through poisonous substances that have been ingested from the Quail's immediate surroundings. If the bird chances upon feed infected with bacteria Clostridium Botulinum, they may contract Botulism, a form of food poisoning that causes weakness, paralysis and death. Other mould and toxic growths may results in such health defects as organ haemorrhage and liver damage. To help keep your Quail safe from unnecessary toxicity, it is best to keep its feed constantly refreshed and stored in dry and airtight conditions at all times.

Chapter 7: Interacting with your Quail

1. Lifting, Holding and Catching your Quail

It doesn't matter if you've been holding your Quail since the day it was born; as an adult, a Quail - especially the New World species - will discourage you from holding them as much as they can. You may wisely want to give your Quail their freedom and not hold them too often, but certain circumstances will require you to lift, hold and even examine the birds for injuries and ailments.

In such situations, it is smart to replicate the calm demeanor of your Quail. Any sudden movements, noise or a large group of people will agitate your Quail and send it scurrying to a hiding spot, or even cause it attempt upward flight. The best way to hold your Quail is to approach it stealthily with a small towel or light blanket. When covered with a blanket, Quail tend to freeze in one spot, and can be picked up without being startled. If you need to hold your Quail in an outdoor setting, it may be best to gently usher it into a corner towards a nesting box or pet carrier.

You may be as stealthy and quiet as a whisper, and still find it next to impossible to catch your Quail - don't be disheartened. Quail are light, fast and precocious birds who take great pride in their ability to evade capture and blend into their natural surroundings. In these cases, create tunnels to enclose the Quails in their nesting boxes using cardboard boxes. Let the tunnels become narrower as the Quail moves through them, till it reaches a point through which it cannot pass. Here, you can gently intervene and lift your Quail.

Lifting your Quail

Once you do manage to approach your Quail, lifting them the right way is of utmost importance. Remember, an adult Quail is significantly larger, heavier and more aggressive than a young one, so its defence tactics are likely to hurt you more. Another point to remember is that Quail cannot be lifted the same way as other domestic birds, such as chickens. Do not attempt to lift them by their feet as they are tiny and delicate; you will cause them severe injury, possibly even a fracture.

The smartest way to lift your Quail is replicate the movements used to grab it as a hatchling. Enclose the body from the sides with your hands in a calm and slow movement. When you lift the bird, its wings should rest neatly and firmly against its body to prevent the Quail from flapping them about either in fight or flight. As your Quail has sharply-tipped feet, you will also need support them by placing a hand beneath its feet. This clasp also prevents the Quail from clawing at you with its toenails.

Whether you leave the Quail's toes dangling from your fingers or fold it under their bodies depends on your preference. Either method of holding the Quail is comfortable for it, provided you don't apply too much pressure.

Once you have finished examining your Quail, place it back down as calmly and gently as you can. Sudden and quick movements may cause the Quail to become agitated and even result in injuries as they land. Understand that some types of Quail, such as the Button Quail or Mountain Quail, may not want to be handled unless absolutely necessary; too much pressure may not only agitate them, but also cause distress to their physical frame.

2. Transporting your Quail

Content though they may be within their cage, you will face many instances during which you may have to transport your Quail to other locations. These may include trips to the local fowl expert, or even longer journeys to the local county fair to compete in quail beauty pageants. Whatever be the circumstance, transporting your Quail comfortably is an issue of importance, as they are easily startled and can also cause both, a mess and a stench in your vehicle. Among the most preferred containers through which to drive your quail around are:

1. Plastic Tubs

Plastic tubs are the cheapest, and also the simplest means through which you can comfortably cart your Quail around. All your transportation tub requires is a short-enough height with a firm roof that prevents the birds from flying upwards when startled. You then drill a few well-placed holes into the roof and the side walls, as a means to facilitate air flow in the tub. Make the floor comfortable and hygienic for the Quail by layering the bottom surface with piles of wood shavings; it will also absorb and hold any wet or waste material produced by your bird. You may also use straw, grass or even strips of newspaper, but these are often less preferred to shavings.

The only factor to keep in mind is that your quail should be as stress-free as possible. Since their stress is often caused by unfamiliar sights or sounds, especially if they are easily frightened, try and provide opaque transportation tubs for your Quail. These will shield your birds away from the outside world, while the dark colours will help them relax. If you must use translucent or transparent-toned plastic tubs, try and cover them with a light cloth to provide some obstacle.

2. Wire Cages

As comfortable as plastic tubs may be, it is the wire cages that are the preferred mode of transportation for Quail owners. It is easy to see why wire cages are highly favoured - with large airy construction, there is little need to drill in your own source of ventilation for the birds. Furthermore, wire cages are easier to carry around and are readily manufactured to suit a variety of needs and preferences. For your Quail, a short cage that measures about 2ft. x 2ft. x 2ft. should be perfect for a pair of even group of four Quail.

While an optimum transportation option in warmer climates, wire cages can quickly become an inconvenience in colder temperatures. The open nature of the cages makes it significantly colder and uncomfortable for the Quail, while also proving a messier affair than their plastic counterparts. With an open free space, it is easy for such particles as stray food, droppings and shedding to simply spill out of the cage. To prevent such mishaps from ruining the upholstery in your vehicle, it is best that you place a plastic sheet under the cage. These cages may also need to be covered up to prevent the Quail from becoming stressed due to a change in the outside environment.

The height of the plastic tub or wire cage is an important factor determining how calm your Quail will be during the journey. In theory, domesticated Quail have a calm enough demeanour that they should not panic easily. However, changing scenery, a constant flow of traffic and unforeseen events may cause your bird to become startled. Short cages not only prevent flight, but also prevent the bird from flapping about the cage and causing a havoc in its panicked state. A tall cage provides the illusion of height and encourages the bird to believe that it can escape the cage, toppling the container in the process.

Tips to ensure safe Quail transportation

1. Secure your transportation container to your vehicle to prevent it from sliding around and causing either stress or a mess. You can do this by buckling the seat belt around the container, or even use heavy-duty straps or bungee cords. This safety measure will ensure that your Quail are not thrown around the vehicle in case of turbulence.

2. Some people say that the odour caused by quail housed together in a small space for long periods of time can become overwhelming during transportation, even causing nausea. Should you find yourself in a similar position, understand that it is perfectly safe to transport Quail in the cargo or exterior storage section of your vehicle; ensure that the tub or cage is firmly attached secured to your vehicle.

3. If you are bringing home newly-hatched Quail from a breeder or vendor and have to transport them over a distance before placing them in incubators on your premises, you can provide heat with a hot-water bottle. Wrap the bottle in a sock or a towel and place within the box in a corner. You can also place the wrapped bottle inside a small resealable plastic bag for additional safety.

4. Try to avoid transporting your Quail with a large group of people, as the noise and crowd may be unsettling for the birds. Loud music and other disturbing behaviour may also cause stress, making the cargo section ideal for peaceful Quail transportation.

5. If you are transporting your Quail over long distances and need to provide feed and water, you can place a large head of lettuce within the container. To prepare the lettuce, simply poke several holes through the lettuce head to reach the centre, and fill up these holes with water. This soaked lettuce head then acts both, as a food and water source for the birds.

6. Finally, ensure that you drive as steadily and responsibly as possible. You do not want to startle and agitate your Quail with rash driving - the results will be loud and unpleasant both for you and the birds!

3. Washing your Quail

As birds that largely care for their own grooming needs, Quail rarely require to be washed, and cleaning the bird on a daily or regular basis is an uncommon practice. In fact, few Quail farmers will invest the labour involved in personally washing each bird in a timely fashion. This does not mean that your Quail should be left to roam with fecal matter splattered across its wings, however.

Quail can, and should ideally, be washed at least once every 7-10 days to help maintain a healthy coat, clean away any parasites that may have settled on their wings, and to wipe away such debris as excess food droppings and stray fecal stains. Regular washing and cleaning is an especially healthy practice if you are rearing your

Quail for exhibition and competitive purposes. To efficiently wash your delicate bird:

1. First, prepare a bowl in which to soak and clean your bird's feathers and body. Choose a wide, yet shallow bowl that will hold the Quail's body comfortably while keeping its head afloat.
2. Fill this bowl with lukewarm water; ensure that the water isn't hot or it will scald your bird's feathers. To this water, add in a teaspoon or two of mild liquid shampoo or soap and mix gently to combine the ingredients. Many farmers find that livestock shampoo such as Ivory works best to clean Quail feathers without damaging the color or health of the coat.
3. To wash your quail, grasp it gently yet firmly, so as not to startle it during the cleaning process. Place a hand under its feet and tuck the feet into its body. Let your index finger rest between the legs, with your thumb and middle finger enclosing each leg within your palm.
4. Lower the quail gently into the soapy water, and wash its feather using your hands or a soft, damp wash cloth. It is essential that you be as gentle as possible, so as not to harm the feathers in any way. Ensure that the bird's head is always above the water to keep it a calm as possible.
5. You will then need a few mugs of clean, fresh water to rinse the soapy particles off the Quail's back and feathers. You can either prepare a separate bowl with clean water and pour this water over the Quail's body, or place the first washing tub near a convenient source of flowing water, such as a running tap or water hose. Around 2-4 mugs of water should be sufficient to wash off any soap scuds and dirty water.
6. Once your Quail has been sufficiently washed, lift it gently and hold it above the bowl for a few seconds to allow excess water to drip off from its body. Enclose the bird in a soft, dry towel and rub each feather dry gently.
7. Once you have wiped away most of the water from the feathers, you can speed up the drying process by holding a

small hair-dryer a little away from the bird's body with the heat turned up to a medium level.

8. Ensure that the hair-dryer is at not point too close to the Quail's feathers, as the heat may cause damage.

4. Pinioning, Wing Clipping and your Quail

Quail require a secure atmosphere in order to be comfortable and stress-free. In some cases, even the most secure and comfortable surroundings may not be enough to stop your Quail from trying to escape. Very often, the only solutions that successfully prevent your Quail from flying away include pinioning and feather clipping.

Pinioning

The process of pinioning requires a trained professional to extract particular section of the bird's wings. By doing so, you take away the bird's ability to fly, which is why this procedure is best undertaken when the Quail are young. Although an effective procedure, pinioning is a painful process and almost always a stressful experience for your Quail. In many instances, pinioning is so traumatic for the Quail that it dies not long after the event.

Not surprisingly, most Quail owners find pinioning to be a cruel and unethical practice. Quite a few locations around the world, in fact, have rendered this practice illegal. Therefore, should you choose to pinion your Quail's wings, ensure that it is allowed and is conducted by an expert in your area. You can also buy Quails whose wings have already been pinioned, if that is your preference.

Feather Clipping

In case pinioning your Quail is not your cup of tea, you can opt for the less painful practice of clipping your Quail feathers. Through this procedure, you cut off the essential features needed for flight, usually only on one side. This makes it difficult for the Quail to fly, although not causing them any harm in the process.

Since it is a painless and simple procedure, most veterinary offices and pet shops will offer feather clipping services at reasonable rates, although you can perform yourself. All you need is one proper training under your waterfowl expert and the dedication to clip your Quail's feather once annually. With a pair of sharp scissors and the knowledge of which feather to clip, you can ensure that that your Quail remains within the premises without causing them trauma.

Are these practices necessary?

Feather clipping and pinioning are only undertaken by those owners who want to prevent their Quails from escaping. As effective as they may be, these acts hinder your Quail's ability to fly even in situations where they need to escape predators.

This is why many Quail owners prefer to leave their Quails' wings untouched, even at the risk of them escaping. A full set of wings allow the Quail to comfortably navigate its surroundings and evade capture from such animals as dogs, raccoon and foxes. Furthermore, a safe and healthy environment filled with other Quails will often be enough to keep the Quail from leaving. The choice to "de-wing" your Quail, or allow them to roam about freely, therefore, is a personal one that requires great thought and consideration for yourself as well as the Quail.

Chapter 8: Health Concerns for Quail

Quail are among the stronger of aviary creatures and have immune systems that can withstand most form of illnesses and infection. They, however, are not infallible, and will become ill and infected if housed in extremely unhygienic conditions. Furthermore, most health-related ailments in Quail are of a nature that can only be isolated and diagnosed through laboratory examinations.

If diagnosed with fatal illnesses past the initial stage of treatment, most Quail, despite their hardy and robust natures, are too small to withstand the physical and emotional trauma that disease or injury may bring. In order to avoid such mishaps from breeding illness among your flock and putting you at a loss, it is best to practice healthy housing and feeding methods that keep sickness at bay.

1.   Common Infections

Coccidiosis

Coccidiosis is a common infection that affects mostly those Quail who are raised and housed in cages that facilitate ground feeding or littering. Caused by a parasite that breeds in unsanitary and damp conditions, this infection manifests itself in the digestive tract of the Quail, making the bird weak and resulting in death if left untreated.

Though Coccidiosis, in theory, can infect any Quail that it comes into contact with, it is generally the younger birds aged between 2 and 6 weeks, along with older birds with significantly weaker immunity, who seem to be affected by the ailment. The hardy and robust anatomy and physiology of the adult Quail provides it with a higher resistance to such infections as Coccidiosis, provided the bird has been raised in optimum conditions.

When infected, Coccidiosis reveals its presence in the Quail's system through such symptoms as sudden loss of appetite, pale appearance and dull feathers, brittle legs and unsteady movements; if left unchecked, these symptoms only become more pronounced with time and may result in the death of the bird. Although healthy adult Quail are less susceptible to this infection, prolonged unhygienic housing and unsanitary feeding conditions may still affect even the most robust bird among your flock; those birds with better immunity, however, will have less aggravated symptoms and may respond to treatments faster and better than their weaker or younger counterparts.

Apart from a dull and listless appearance, a coccidiosis infection can easily be spotted in the droppings shed by your Quail. Some forms of this infection may result in droppings with blood from the infected intestinal lining mixed into them; others, in the absence of blood, will be coated with a slimy, mucus membrane. In the event that your Quail has died of a Coccidiosis infection, you can observe the manifestation of his ailment by dissecting the intestinal tract of the bird during a necropsy.

Those Quail who are infected with the cocci will generally take between 10 to 14 days to recover, based on the treatment provided to them. Most commonly, Coccidiosis can be treated by adding medicines that contain the ingredient coccidiostat which helps kill of cocci. The most popularly used treatments are Sulmet (Sulfamethazine) and Corid (Amprolium), medications available in both liquid and powder form at most online veterinary pharmacies and local animal hospitals.

To treat your Quail, measure 9.5 cc of Corid and mix it into the water feeders provided for your Quail. If you choose to use Sulmet, begin with 2 tablespoons of the medicine in the drinking water for the first 2 days, and then lower the dosage to 1 tablespoon for the next 4 days. Sulmet is known to be relatively stronger than Corid and will need to stop for about a week after the 6-day dosage period, to allow recovery.

Ensure that the feeders are clean and filled with fresh water before adding the medications. Change the water once daily and continue treatment for up to 2 weeks, till the affected birds have regained their health. If your Quail have higher immunity or has already built a resistance to the infection, they may take a shorter time to recover and resume egg-productivity within a few days.

If Coccidiosis has affected your younger birds, you can provide them with medicated feed that contains added Amprolium; however, only provide this feed to those young Quail who have not been vaccinated against this ailment. Amprolium can also be added in smaller doses to the water of all Quail birds, as a preventive and immunity-building measure against Coccidiosis.

The infection itself can be cleaned away from the bedding, by either changing the flooring within the pen entirely, or by treating the flooring with ammonia. Known to effectively kill away cocci, Quail should be cleared away from the infected area before treating the ground with 10% ammonia solution mixed with water.

As a natural treatment, Apple Cider Vinegar has been found to be useful not only at flushing the parasite out of the Quail's system, but also in building up tolerance against the infection itself. A natural antibacterial and disinfectant, 1 tablespoon of Apple Cider Vinegar mixed in the drinking water of your Quail and changed daily, will help keep your flock healthy and Coccidiosis-free.

Quail Disease

As a Quail farmer or owner, Ulcerative Enteritis, or Quail Disease as it commonly known, is perhaps the infection that has the highest probability of striking your flock. As with coccidiosis, Quail Disease is an infection of the intestinal tract that may be contracted by the younger birds in your flock; if left untreated, however, this infection can turn deadly within a short span of time and result in the loss a majority or even the entirety of your flock.

In a manner that is similar to Coccidiosis, Quail Disease is also seen to be contracted largely by those Quail who have been reared directly on the ground or among litter. This is not to say that wire-reared Quail will never contract Quail Disease; simply that the risk of exposure to the bacteria may be lower. This infection is seen to have been brought in not only by the droppings and contaminated feed in your housing areas, but also by new birds added to the flock, whether or same breed or another species.

Quail Disease requires immediate treatment for full recovery; an infected Quail will die within 2 days if left untreated. Your Quail will display a variety of symptoms that points towards its ill health, from listless behaviour, loss of appetite, drooping feathers and a shabby coat, to watery and partially closed eyes, diarrhoea, a retracted neck and loose, watery stool that may appear ashen or even chalky white. The downside of these symptoms is that they can be indicative of nearly any infection in Quail; Ulcerative enteritis is only determined by submitting a sample of your bird's stool for medical examination.

If a Quail in your flock has died due to this infection, you can also conduct a necroscopy to properly study the appearance of Ulcerative Enteritis in the bird. You should find ulcers and lesions along the intestine, along with yellow mucus-membranes and blood and fluid in the intestine. Since immediate treatment is necessary for a partial or complete recovery of your flock, a sick or dead Quail within your group may signal an already spreading infection and a need for urgent medical attention.

Upon detection, those Quail with Ulcerative Enteritis are best isolated from your healthy flock. If you suspect that the infection may have attacked the entire flock, it is wise to change their housing location immediately and begin treatment. A dosage 1 tablespoon of Duramycin is to be added immediately to a gallon of drinking water and provided to the flock for 7-14 days, or until the flock has made a complete recovery. Another easily available treatment is Streptomycin, of which 44 gms is to be added to 100 litres of water before administering to the Quail. Medications such as Duramycin and Streptomycin are known to be strong in their effect and will affect the quality of the meat and eggs that you receive from the Quail; these should be withdrawn for a period of 21 days after administering the last treatment to your birds.

Chronic Respiratory Disease

Chronic Respiratory Disease, also known as Mycoplasma Gallisepticum, is generally known to affect those Quail who have been introduced to a new flock member – especially if the flock member has been acquired from the wild. This bacterial infection affecting the respiratory tract of Quail can also be transmitted by other poultry such as chickens, and is best prevented through such smart practices as quarantining new flock members for a probation period.

When afflicted with Chronic Respiratory Disease, your Quail may look as though they have a very bad cold; symptoms of this infection include runny and watery eyes, possibly foamy residue around the eye area, runny nose and inflamed nostrils, accompanied by coughs and sneezing. To treat the ailment, Duramycin administered in dosage of 1 tablespoon in a gallon of water should help treat the infection; however, it may not be able to prevent your bird from becoming a carrier of the disease. It is for this reason that those Quail affected with Chronic Respiratory Disease are isolated from the rest of the flock, and sometime even put to rest.

Bumblefoot

Wire cages are often considered – and quite rightly so – to be a preferred form of housing for your flock of Quail as it lowers their risk of exposure to several forms of bacterial and viral infections. Their efficiency at minimizing infections among your flock, however, does not prevent them from being an uncomfortable surface upon which to perch on for long hours. Prolonged periods of standing and movement on narrow wire surfaces can cause injuries to the sensitive feet of Quail, resulting in infections that cause a condition known as Bumblefoot.

Quail feet, especially the pads on the undersides, are known to be extremely sensitive in addition to being tiny in size; factors such as long durations of standing, small pieces of broken wire or sharp edges can easily cause damage and open up the skin to infections. Once the infection begins in the foot, it quickly spreads to other parts of the body, eventually killing the bird if left untreated.

If affected with Bumblefoot, your quail will display such symptoms as excessively red and swollen feet; freshly bruised feet may be tender to the touch, while slightly older wounds must also develop a crusty, hard coating. The most obvious indication of Bumblefoot among your birds, however, is a pronounced limp in their gait, accompanied by a reluctance to walk on the wire. If you examine the pads under the feet, you may even spot the root of the infection through a black spot on the pad.

Infections caused due to Bumblefoot can be directly removed from larger birds such as turkeys or chickens; this, however, is a near-impossible process with birds as small as Quail. It is for this reason that preventing the possibility of Bumblefoot is far wiser than treating the ailment, should it occur.

As soon as your Quail exhibits signs of Bumblefoot, it is best to place them on a floor that is heavily layered with soft piles of bedding. This immediate relief for their feet should be followed by a foot soak in an Epsom salt bath for 10 to 15 minutes once or twice daily. The Epsom salts should help to soothe the inflammation and draw out most of the infection; follow this soak with a liberal application of Neosporin around the affected area.

If you manage to catch the infection and treat it early, your Quail should make a complete recovery within a week. If left unsupported or ignored for too long, the infection may spread too far into the system to treat with Epsom salt or Neosporin. In an ideal housing environment, health concerns such as Bumblefoot should rarely – if at all- occur among your Quail. To best prevent its occurrence among your flock, ensure that the cages are provided with plenty of nooks and spots with soft bedding for a break from the rough wire surface.

Head Boink

Although not a medical or technical term, Head Boink – as comical as it may sound – is an unwanted health concern that can abruptly cause injury and trauma, and even result in the untimely death of your bird. Not caused by an infection or disorder in the system, a Head Boink is caused when your startled or frightened bird makes an abrupt flight upwards and hurts its head on the roof of the cage. The resulting damage to the head, neck and spine of the Quail often impairs its movement and can prove fatal to its mortality.

1. Head injury caused due to startled flight will likely occur among your Quail in the instances that they have been frightened. From predatory attacks, to fights within the flock, to even improper handling of the bird on your part, a number of factors may result in the abrupt injury of the bird. Owing to their small size and the disproportionately large amount of damage caused, there is little you can do by way of treatment, except provide immediate nursing and individual attention.

2. A Quail who has hit their head against the roof of the cage will often be unsteady and wobbly in their movements; in some cases, a severe injury may even cause them to look paralyzed or seem disoriented. As soon as you spot such behaviour, it is best to take the Quail out from the cage and place it in isolation. An injured Quail will immediately enter a state of shock and develop early stages of hypothermia; you may have to prevent this by placing the Quail near a heating source, such as a heating lamp or hot water bottle placed near the bird's body.

3. Ensure that your bird is as comfortable as possible by providing layers of bedding and placing water and food at its immediate disposal. You will have to provide water by dipping the bird's beak directly into the bowl at regular intervals; food will have to be deposited in the bird's

mouth or hand-fed. For a game bird such as Quail, there is sadly little else that can be done by way of treating a head injury.

4. If your Quail has received only superficial damage to its head, neck or spine, it should recover within a span of 7 days; if your pet is still in pain and discomfort after a week, it may be best to have it put down to avoid a painful and slow death.

2.   Other ailments

Apart from the above mentioned conditions that may befall your Quail, here are some ailments that may affect your flock if housed in improper conditions:

Name of disease	Definition	Symptoms	Treatment
Egg binding	inability among hens to pass egg due to injury to vagina, abnormal size of egg, or calcium deficiency, among other causes	difficulty in egg laying, nervous disposition, agitation, depression, abnormal gait or body posture, abrupt death	Immediate assistance from veterinarian, increase in calcium in Quail diet
Capillary Worm Infection	infection of the crop tissue by crop and capillary worms, caused due to unhygienic housing conditions	thickening of crop wall, starved appearance of birds, presence of threadlike worms in	Raise Quail on wire, clean feeders and water feeders, raise all Quail equipment 3-6 inches off ground,

		infected crop, sudden mortality	disinfect premises Immediate assistance from veterinarian for deworming medication
Other worm infections	Red worm and Tapeworm infections	Drop in egg production, abrupt increase in appetite, diarrhoea	Immediate assistance from veterinarian for deworming medication
Mites	ailment caused due to constant feeding on Quail by Red and Northern mites, among others, caused in an unhygienic housing environment	lowered egg production, pale appearance, scabs around face and vent, appearance of mites around vent,	Use specialised mite-spray on premises dissolve 6.5 fluid ounces of 10% Permethrin Ec in 10 gallons water and spray on the vent area of Quail once, and used around housing every few months, inspect housing area every month at night for presence of mites
Coryza	fatal bacterial disease	swelling of	keep chicken at

	transmitted through to Quail	face, heavy and ragged breathed, thick and foul discharge from eyes and nose, labored sounds from lungs while breathing	least 20 feet away from quail at all times, do not mix chicken with quail in nesting space, wear different clothes and wash hands before handling Quail, 1 teaspoon Sulfadimethoxine per gallon of water for 5-6 days, refreshed daily
Histomoniasis	Protozoan disease caused due to the interaction of parasite with liver causing damage, carried often by chickens and other poultry birds	loss of appetite, listless behavior, yellowish droppings, abrupt mortality	no approved treatment for the disease, practice biosecurity measures, keep chicken at least 20 feet away from quail at all times, do not mix chicken with quail in nesting space, wear different clothes and wash hands before handling Quail

Quail Bronchitis	fatal disease caused mainly in Bobwhites due to infection contracted from wild birds	rattled breathing, inflammation of the eye and coughing	no treatment for the disease, accompanying ailments can be treated with 1 teaspoon Tylan powder per gallon water in for 4-5 days, refreshed daily

3.   Quail and Behavioural Issues

Many breeds of Quail, especially the Old World breeds, can be very social and placid creatures if housed in spacious quarters and in the correct sex ratio. If you do observe any sudden behavioral changes in your Quail, these can be attributed to two major factors - a change in the Quails' surroundings or within the bird's personalities themselves.

Just as adolescents undergo a form of identity crisis just before maturation, so do some Quail face behavioral issues, usually preceding their first sexual encounter with a hen. This behaviour will often signal your Quails' progress from a juvenile Quail to an adult Quail ready for mating. Behavioral changes to watch out for during this period include pecking, pinching, short bursts of charging, and generally hostile behavior.

Perturbing though this behavior may be, understand that you can calm your Quail down and teach them to keep a check on their aggressive tendencies. Quail are intelligent and perceptive enough that a sharp reprimand from you in a consistent tone of voice every time they behave badly will send a clear message. Try and use the same word and gesture to admonish your Quail, such as "no" or "stop". Accompany this phrase with a subtly dominant gesture, such as holding your Quail gently by the back of its neck till it and placing it in a separate bag till it is calm.

These acts of dominance should never aim to hurt your Quail; simply let them know they're being unreasonable. Quail, especially cockerels, tend to view all bigger living beings as competition or threats, so it is important to reassure them that you are neither. By kindly yet firmly asserting your authority, you can win over their trust and loyalty in no time.

The only other critical change in Quail behavioral patterns occur when they undergo periods of severe stress. Ranging from reasons such as a change in the temperature to the arrival of new Quail, and even including serious health concerns, any abrupt difference in the behaviour of a Quail may cause it to display such stressful symptoms as loss of appetite, shallow breathing and isolation from other members of the flock. Any such significant differences in behavior are causes for worry and should be addressed with your fowl expert immediately.

4.   The Importance of Veterinary Care

Experienced and professional though they may be, veterinarians for animals such as cats, dogs, rabbits, hamsters etc. may not always be the best people to treat your Quail. These ground-dwelling aviary creatures require special care from poultry experts who have specialized in and are more familiar with the health requirements of your Quail. The good news is, finding a Quail health expert is an easy-enough process.

If you do not already have a veterinary expert to contact, your Quail sellers, retailers or breeders will all be happy to help you. Breeders and retailers usually have the best sources on call, since the health of their Quails is their top priority. If these options don't work out for you, however, some simple research of your own will yield plenty of results.

Many experts offering poultry and gamebird health care services advertise on the Internet and can be located within a few minutes. Additionally, you can also rely on feedback and reviews from other Quail breeders and owners to narrow down the best option for your Quail.

Once you find your fowl expert, it is best to take your Quail up to them for an initial examination. To help avoid exposing your Quails as to prolonged interaction with strangers or unhygienic conditions, try to find an expert who is willing to make house calls, especially if you own a flock of Quail. Many experts understand the relative complications involved in transporting a large flock in a cramped vehicle, and are more than willing to oblige you.

5.   Treating attacks from predators

Quail have a few tricks at their disposal to help them evade capture from predators in their area. Furthermore, if you have provided the right kind of nesting and sheltering spaces, your Quail should be at minimum risk of harm. Despite your best efforts, however, you may not always be able to avoid predatory attacks.

Predatory Terrain	Common Predators
Terrestrial predators	Snakes, foxes, dogs, wolves, coyotes, weasels, minks, bobcats, opossums ,raccoons, dingoes, skunks, rats, badgers, ferrets, cats, bears
Aerial predators	Hawks, falcons, owls, crows, ravens, magpies,
Marine predators	Otters, herons, turtles, crocodiles, frogs, large fish

If your Quail is not able to escape or is not defended by a bigger creature, there are high possibilities that they may not survive the attack. Often, such injuries as a severed neck, internal bleeding, a ruptured organ, or even the trauma of the attack turn out to be life-threatening for the bird. In the instance that your bird has survived the attack, and has received immediate attention, they can overcome the intensity of the injury with the right care.

The first step you have to take is provide first-aid for the bird's wounds. Your waterfowl expert will recommend that you stock an antibacterial wash for the injuries; use this to clean the affected areas. If you do not have any wash at hand, clean water will suffice. During this wash, gently check your Quail for any fractures, sprains, or injuries that may seem even slightly painful. Address these concerns by either taking the bird to the fowl expert at once, or asking them to make an urgent house visit.

Your veterinarian will be able to repair most injuries caused due to predatory attacks. Once his job is done, it is up to you and your Quail to ensure that your pet makes a complete recovery. During the healing stage, these birds are highly vulnerable to infections and post-traumatic stress. To help them recover, try and provide as sterile and comfortable an atmosphere as you can. Coordinate with your fowl expert to determine the time of recovery, means of medication and any other factors that can aid your bird's rehabilitation. No matter how traumatic the attack, it is your response to the event that can help save your Quail's life.

6.   Treating a Broken Wing

A Quail takes great pride in its wings, viewing it as an integral part of the Quail's identity. A broken wing, therefore, is arguably one of the most traumatic episodes that a Quail may experience. Injury to the Quail's wing inhibits such routine activities as walking, running or even standing, causing great stress to its well-being. And if you are a Quail owner who is ethically against practices like pinioning or feather clipping, understand that wing injury can be as adversely impactful as these methods.

If your Quail has not already signalled an injury with distress calls, you can spot an injured wing for yourself by its appearance. When injured, a Quail's wing tends to hang on the Quail's body at an odd, drooping angle. You will also find that the broken wing is visibly asymmetrical to the wing on the other side.

A broken or injured wing could be caused due to a variety of reasons, the most common of them being aggressive behavior among the flock. Male Quail especially will look to damage their competitors' wings to gain dominance during the breeding and mating season. Sometimes, these acts of aggression can become so uncontrollable that male Quail will accidentally injure the female in their rush to be the first to mate with her.

If all is well among your Quail, a broken wing could then be traced to a predatory attack. Used as a powerful tool of defence and evasion, it is the wings that predators look to attack in order to maim and weaken a Quail. Other anomalies such as tears and cuts in the wire fencing, or stray sharp tree branches may also injure the Quail's wing.

No matter how your Quail may have been hurt, as soon as you spot an injured wing, inform your waterfowl expert in order to get your Quail immediate attention. While you wait for this medical assistance, there are steps you can take to help calm your Quail, stabilize the wound and prevent the injury from worsening:

1. To provide first-aid to your Quail, you have to calm it down and convince it to take your help. An injured Quail reacts to this stressful event by becoming extremely hostile, and will not want to be held or handled.

2. To calm your Quail down, gain their trust by placing their feed and fresh water within easy reach, and give the Quail some space. When the Quail begins feeding, it is usually a safe sign that the Quail has calmed down enough that it can be approached.

3. Not all Quails are as easily pacified. In many cases, your Quail will refuse to stay still due to its distress and in these instances, the only way to calm your Quail is to lift it yourself. Remember, your Quail has an injured wing, and so

will not move as efficiently as usual. Use this advantage to gently corner your Quail so you can lift and examine its wing.

4. The best spots to corner your Quail are ones in which he will calm down easily. Such spots include nesting and feeding zones - areas familiar to the Quail.

5. When you do lift your Quail, hold the injured side away from your body, and gingerly inspect the wing area for visible tears or lacerations.

6. Any wounds that you do spot should be cleaned immediately. You can use the antibacterial wash suggested by your fowl expert, or even opt for an iodine wash or a bath with mildly warm water.

7. In case your fowl expert does not arrive by this point, or you have to address the injury yourself, you must prepare yourself to create a small makeshift splint for your Quail's wing. This is to help your Quail receive some support for its wing while it recovers.

8. The most important reason behind providing support for the wing is to help it heal back to its earlier state. For this you have to gently hold the wing back in its natural position against your Quail's body. It is important that your touch be as painless as possible.

9. Now, get out a roll of gauze and wrap it's securely around your Quail enclosing the wing within. When you bring the gauze over the other side, wrap it under the uninjured wing. This will allow the Quail to have some kind of control over its movement and help lower its stress levels.

10. You can fasten the gauze with pieces of strong tape, or even wrap a layer of tape around the gauze to ensure that its stays put.

11. While the purpose of the gauze and tape is to prevent the Quail from moving its wing, ensure that you don't wrap it on too tightly. This may constrict the Quail's body and make it difficult for the Quail to breathe.

12. Quail with injured wings recover best when kept in nesting zones by themselves. They will make a full recovery in about 2-3 weeks, provided you give keep them fed and rested.

13. You may notice that the protective gauze has become dirty or soiled; you can change the dressing if you wish. Usually, owners will change the dressing after the first week or two. If you take off the dressing during this point and find your Quail exercising its wing comfortably, take it to mean that your pet has healed.

14. Once the Quail is flapping and waddling about confidently, they will automatically socialize with the others in their flock. This is a healthy sign that your Quail has made a complete recovery.

Not all wing injuries may be this procedural or easy to fix. In case the wound looks too deep, or has been caused due to a predatory attack, it is best that you seek immediate help from your veterinarian.

7.   Quail and the Moulting Phenomenon

The feathers on a Quail's body function in a manner similar to the hair on human skin or the fur on Quailian bodies. Appendages that are comprised mainly of a protein compound called keratin, feathers are inherently "dead" by nature and extend outward from the bird's body as a means of protection and adornment.

Part of a continuous cycle of growth, shedding and re-emergence, the feathers on a Quail's body shed and fall off to make way for new, healthy feathers, just as human or mammalian hair would. The shedding period among Quail, however, is not a subtle

91

process that occurs on a daily basis. It is during the months between August and December that Quail generally shed their feathers to make way for new ones. As an amateur Quail or poultry farmer, you may not have witnessed an abrupt "balding" of your birds, with feathers scattered across the cage. Do not be alarmed; this process, that occurs once or even twice among certain Quail breeds, is known as moulting.

The reason for the occurrence of moulting is fairly straightforward. In the wild, Quail generally occupy the warmer months between February and July with breeding and egg-laying activity. Since the production of eggs requires a high amount of protein and other nutrients essential for the maintenance of feathers, Quail tend to prioritise egg-laying over cosmetic appearance in the summer months.

With the arrival of the winter months however, Quail witness a shift in physiological priorities and realign their hormonal activity towards providing nourishment for their feathers. This switch in the distribution of nutrients results in damaged feathers shedding from the bird's body, subsequently replaced with fresh feathers within as little as 2 weeks. In order to help facilitate the appearance of a healthy plumage, egg-production will see a slight drop as a result; once the plumage has been recovered; however, your Quail's egg-laying habits to resume to normal.

If you do not wish for your Quail's egg-laying abilities to be hindered by the moulting phenomenon, it may be smartest to trick the Quail into believing its cooler months are, in fact, an extension of the summer. It is shorter hours of daylight and cooler temperatures that bring about moulting in Quail; maintaining the summer temperature in the winter months and providing 17 hours of light on daily basis, along with added calcium and minerals for egg health will help keep a moulting incident at bay.

8. Preventing Health Concerns among your Quail

Since most infections and ailments that befall your Quail often manifests among unsanitary housing conditions, diseases, especially in Quail are best prevented, rather than treated. In spaces that house several types of poultry together, Quail should be kept separate from such species as turkeys, and particularly chickens, who are ready carriers of bacterial parasites. The Quail themselves are best housed on wire with enough space separating the wire floor from the bedding on the ground. Here are a few other tips to ensure that the spread and contraction of illnesses among your flock are kept to a minimum:

- Regular check-ups of the cage for lice, mites and other parasites and clean the housing quarters with insecticide solution
- Replace feed in the cage within 15 days of placing in the feeder; old feeding bowls filled with uncleaned food particles will become damp, mouldy and cause illnesses.
- Water feeders will have to be changed and cleaned on a daily basis
- Reserve a pair of clothing and shoes specifically for Quail farming purposes. Ensure that clothes and shoes are cleaned after each interaction; disinfected after interaction with sick birds.
- Ensure that such activities as handling, breeding and egg hatching are undertaken by as few people as possible; introducing the birds or eggs to several humans at once increases the risk of spread of infection among all involved parties.

9.   Meat and Egg Withdrawal during Medication and Treatment

As birds that contract severe strains of bacterial and viral infections should ailments befall them, Quail require medications and a treatment program comprising chemical compositions that may effectively treat the birds, but may be harmful to the human body upon contact. Such medications as Duramycin, Streptomycin and the like, if present in the eggs or meat of the Quail at the time of sale, render the products unfit for human consumption. Not only does this situation put the Quail owner at a financial loss, but is also considered a breach of poultry farming regulations set by Wildlife governing authorities.

To prevent the medications used to treat broiler and layer breeds from causing health concerns among the humans that purchase and consume them, governing authorities in several countries including the United States and United Kingdom place a "meat and egg withdrawal" period on the produce of many breeds of poultry, livestock and cattle.

According to this meat and egg withdrawal principle, those poultry and livestock that are treated with medicated feeds or medicines for specific ailments should refrain from providing either their meat or eggs from the last medicated dose until a date by which the medicines would have left the animals' bodies. The duration of the meat or egg withdrawal may differ among the medicines and the species of animals; the average duration of withdrawal stipulated by the UK government is 21 days for meat and eggs of Quail. Most poultry health experts, however, will be able to allot a suitable and reasonable withdrawal period for the produce of your Quail, should it require medication.

10. Providing insurance for your Quail

Birds such as Quail are relatively easy to care for and have been blessed with a hardy disposition; but also require an environment that is both hygienic and secure. A clean, comfortable and safe housing space keeps them protected against injury and harm from predators, or from contracting illnesses that arise in an inhospitable housing zone.

Despite your best intentions, you may not always be able to guarantee that a raccoon or fox won't slip through loose wiring and snatch a Quail, or you may not have foreseen a viral or bacterial infection that has plagued members of your flock. It is perhaps because of reasons like these, that when Quail do succumb to illnesses, they are often of a recurring nature and require long-term medical and supportive care. A Quail who contracts a respiratory infection may have a weak immune system and may be constantly susceptible to infections; another pet with an egg binding defect may constantly need medical and nutritional attention. When combined with other factors such as untimely death or theft of the bird from the premises, it seems like a variety of factors could contribute towards you losing your Quail.

To help protect you financially, countries like the United States and the United Kingdom offer health and livestock insurance policies for pets of many varieties, including birds such as Quail. Healthcare and medical plans chalked up by these companies provide an umbrella of financial cover for such cases as medical ailments, death due to accidents, destruction or natural causes, theft or kidnapping of flock or individual bird, and providing transit cover for your flock in case of long-haul transportation.

In the United States, pet insurance policies are offered by such companies as The Hartford and Markel Animal Mortality. In the United Kingdom, you can find pet insurance policies with companies like Crowe Livestock and LRMS Insurance.

The insurance company Catlin, on the other hand, offers attractive insurance policies across offices in the United Kingdom, Canada, Asia Pacific and Australia.

Chapter 9: The Practice of Breeding Quail

When you have made the time and found the resources to breed Quail for a profit, you come across another important decision - the choice to opt for birds born through natural or artificial breeding methods.

Through the natural breeding method, Quail will only breed with members of their own type, in order to maintain a pure genetic code. Through the process of natural selection, however, Quail species over the years have undergone subtle genetic mutations to adapt their bodies evolving environments. When you breed Quail through the natural method, you allow nature to play its part in determining which traits in your birds are desirable, and which can be eliminated.

You may also opt for artificial breeding, an increasingly popular method of Quail breeding today. This school of breeding gives you control over the traits that you would want your flock to possess. However, successful mutation is an intricate and complicated process, and does not always ensure the results you wished for. Since physical traits seem to be the characteristics most affected by artificial breeding, this option is sensible should you choose to breed Quail for exhibitionary and display purposes.

1.   Breeding Quail for Exhibition

If your intent for raising the Quails is to acquire their meat and eggs for commercial use, the plumage and physical appearance of the Quail will make no actual difference to the nature of care they require. If you are bringing home and raising Quail for decorative, exhibition or competitive purposes, however, you will be especially interested in the physical appearance, breed and even lineage of the Quail.

While wild Quail have a distinctively coloured plumage that has been ascertained through centuries of natural breeding, science has allowed Quail enthusiasts to breed Quail by intermingling species for results that are equally beautiful, yet completely individualistic. Since the endless possibilities that breeding provides may give an unfair advantage to some experienced individuals over others, most poultry associations that judge decorative competitions only accept those Quail with their natural colorings. For exhibition and personal pleasures, however, you can choose from increasingly diverse range of available Quail breeds.

A drawback of having diverse color patterns among Quail is the confusion that arises when they are to be identified. If you plan on bringing home Quail, it is important that you have a basic understanding of the role that genetic factors play in determining the appearance of these birds.

2.   Genetics and consequent Quail appearance

The DNA structure in living beings controls every aspect of development - from physical traits, to mental progress and even emotional tendencies. Quail are not exempt from this natural phenomenon, and pass down inherent characteristics embedded into their genetic codes through the generations.

Because the physical coats of Quail are so diversely patterned and colored, the genetic structure of their code can be modified to produce different results in subsequent Quail generations. Through these modifications, breeders have the option of emphasising those traits that they find desirable, while submitting those traits that they find negative or unwelcome.

The process of genetic modification does not only take place in the laboratories; this is a natural evolutionary process that has resulted in contemporary wild New World breeds. Abrupt abnormalities in genetic mutations can also occur when an entire flock or more of Quails are affected by a similar tweak in their code.

In order to pass down genetic traits that determine plumage, behaviour patterns and physical characteristics, the sex cells of each parent fuse to provide half the structure required for the genetic code of the hatchling. A Quail hatchling, therefore, will contain a gene copy received from the mother and father. Since the final cell is fused using only half of the parent genes, the hatchling's cell may either be composed of two similar cells - making them homozygous, or two different cells - rendering them heterozygous.

It is this homozygous or heterozygous nature that determines the spread and distribution of physical and sexual traits in the hatchling. If the hatchling carries similar versions of both cells, it will naturally display the dominant traits it has received. If the hatchling receives two different genes codes, however, it will display the mutations of the more dominant set of traits, resulting in a variety of physical patterns and colorations.

3.   Breeding Quail according to your preference

With this basic understanding of DNA and patterns of inheritance, you can begin breeding your own generations of Quail with color patterns that suit your preferences. As a beginner level breeder, you may want to purchase your first group of Quail from a reputed professional; they will be able to provide you with birds that possess a superior breeding.

You will have to ensure that the birds you select for breeding are free of health ailments, deformities and are not carriers of any infection. You will also want to select those Quail that possess the optimum physical characteristics - ideal weight, size and coloring - along with a pleasing disposition. Finally, you may choose to bring home Quail eggs and hatch them yourself; if this be the case, ensure that the eggs you select meet the necessary requisites in terms of color, shape and weight; if the egg you pick is thin-shelled, brittle, under or even overweight, you may not hatch a Quail of the highest breeding.

No.	Color	Inheritance	Characteristic Manifestation	Examples
1.	Extended Brown/Black	Autosomal Incomplete Dominant	Extended black/brown pigmentation across torso of the bird, same in both sexes	British Range. English White, Tuxedo
2.	Recessive White	Autosomal Recessive	When homozygous: White bird with dark eyes When heterozygous:Two-color "Tuxedo" pattern with white ventral surface, neck and face, with black/brown dorsal surface	English White, Tuxedo, British Range (can also take on Tuxedo coloring), Texas A&M
3.	Yellow/Golden	Autosomal Dominant	Rich golden, hay or straw colored hue with similar to wild Japanese Quail, however, spread of pigmentation is wider than wild birds, seen across wing bow and head feathers	Manchurian Golden
4.	Dilute	Sex-linked Recessi	Causes reduction in pigmentation without affecting eye color Lightly colored down and	Fawn, Cinnamon

		ve	plumage, shank is usually without pigmentation	
5.	Imperfect albinism	Sex-linked Recessive	High levels of pigmentation in the eyes and feather coloring Faint stripes on backs of adults Reduced viability in homozygous Quail	-
6.	Redhead/ Breasted	Autosomal Recessive	Charred black under fluff with white feathers at the base containing black or grey coloring, whitish breast, back, abdomen, flank and shank, black/rust feather tips, white head with black/rust rings Males darker than females in general	Button,
7.	Red	Autosomal		Red Golden. Scarlett, Roux Dilute, Red Range
8.	White beard	Autosomal Recessive	Small white beard-like patch under lower beak on brown Quail	Pharoah (wild), Jumbo Brown

9.	White Breasted	Autosomal Recessive	White feathers covering face, neck, breast, primary and other feathers, sternum and vent	Bobwhite
10.	White crescent	Autosomal Recessive	White-feathered band in a crest shaped patterns extending across breast of brown Quail	-
11.	White Primaries	Autosomal Recessive	White primary feathers with colored body	Pharoah (wild)
12.	Fawn	Co-dominant to Yellow	Golden colored hue seen across wing bow and head feathers	Golden Manchurian, Italian
13.	Blue	Recessive	Replaces brown coloring for bluish-grey Replaces cream colorings for white	Mountain, California, Button
14.	Recessive Silver	Autosomal Recessive	Mate homozygous male with heterozygous female to reproduce May affect egg-laying abilities in homozygotic female	-
15.	Silver	Incomplete		

		Domin ant		

4. Advantages of Breeding Quail

1. Quail breeding and farming is a relatively economical venture to invest in, when compared to other forms of animal husbandry.
2. As small-sized birds, quail do not require vast expanses of land for farming; a group of 6 quail can be reared with ease within an area measuring 1 metre sq – the same amount of space required for 1 chicken.
3. With a gentle disposition harboured by many breeds, particularly the Old-World quail species, they are easier to handle than other birds such as chickens or Quail.
4. Their pleasing and social natures, along with little need for individual attention also keeps labor costs low; as an amateur quail farmer raising a small group of birds, you may rarely require extra assistance.
5. Feeding a group of quail costs less than providing regular feed for birds such as chickens or Quail; with a 12 kilogram bag of feed costs only about 20 USD.
6. Quail farming is particularly advantageous for those who chose this endeavor to make a profit from the eggs. Adult female Coturnix quail begin laying eggs at 6-7 weeks of age with a hatching period that last no longer than 18 days.
7. In their first year as layers, healthy adult female quail can supply up to 300 eggs, with an only slightly lowered rate of productivity in the following years.
8. As a quail farmer, you benefit from a higher conversion rate of feed to meat or eggs than birds such as chickens or Quail would provide. As cost-efficient birds, quail will require only 3 kilograms of feed to produce around 1 kilogram of meat or eggs.

9. Quail also possess an arguably more robust disposition than their chicken, pheasant or Quail counterparts. They can adapt to a variety of environments and are less prone to ailments and infections.

10. The ease of breeding and farming quail as a business is considered so low-maintenance compared to rearing other birds, that many quail small and medium-scale quail farmers have been able to manage a thriving business without sacrificing their primary means of employment.

11. Along with being easy to care for and efficient in their supply of meat and eggs, the demand for quail and quail produce in the food market makes quail breeding and farming a highly-profitable venture with quick turnarounds; with a small group of quail bred primarily for eggs, you can earn up to in your first year alone.

Chapter 10: Caring for Quail Eggs and Young

1.   Features of a Quail Egg

The quality of your Quail egg depends on a variety of factors ranging from the environment your bird lives to the nutritional content of its feed. Provided that you raise your flock of Quail in the right conditions, the average Quail egg should have a smooth, unblemished shell whose color will be between range between a smooth pale brown to pale blue-grey color with brown or blue-grey speckles. A healthy egg should weigh between 8 and 13 grams, with ideal hatching weight being 10 grams.

Whether you choose to sell the Quail eggs for a profit, or use them to replenish your own food source, understand that Quail eggs provide high levels of nutrition. A Quail egg is a bountiful source of vitamins and minerals as vitamins A, B6, B12, D, E, iron, potassium, phosphorous, calcium and zinc. In addition, a Quail egg provides essential amino acids and healthy Omega-rich fats, essential for daily sustenance. Finally, a Quail egg provides between 100 and 10 calories of your daily intake, while supplying you with protein and a little over 600 mg of healthy.

2.   Dealing with the Eggs

Quail are generally ready to lay eggs by the time they are six to eight weeks old if they are layer Coturnix breeds; a little longer with other breeds. If you have provided the right nesting conditions, a Quail hen will either drop her eggs wherever she sees fit, or select preferred spots and begin to lay an egg per day almost immediately. What happens with the eggs from that point is your choice to make.

You have one of two options to choose at this stage - either allow the eggs to hatch into hatchlings or use the eggs as a food source for profit or personal use. Initially, many Quail breeders choose to simply observe how their Quail interact, mate, lay, incubate and hatch their eggs. This is a wise option, as it allows you to study and determine how you'd like to use the eggs based on the yield and breed.

You may not want to breed the Quail you have or use their eggs for any purpose. This is perfectly fine, but it will also require some work on your part to prevent the eggs from hatching. If making an egg nonviable is your choice, stay alert to the time that your Quail leaves its laying spot each day to wash and feed itself. When she is busy, make your way to the eggs, lift and shake each one, before placing them back.

The act of shaking the egg damages the delicate contents and blood vessels within, putting a stop to the development process. To prevent your Quail form further laying eggs, it is essential that you place the shaken eggs back in place. If your Quail can't find her eggs upon return, she'll simply lay a fresh batch.

3.   Collecting the eggs for breeding

If you have provided the right incubation conditions for your Quail, expect to be pleasantly surprised with the yield! At the peak of the breeding season, you will get up to 4, even more eggs per female Quail per day. This yield, at the end of the laying season can total up to a healthy average of 300 Quail eggs a year! It is important to understand, however, that attaining all the eggs that have been laid may not always be possible. A variety of factors determine how many eggs you can actually collect and how many of these can be either sold or hatched successfully.

If collecting the Quail eggs is your goal, remember that the Quail may not lay eggs at their nests alone. In a comfortable atmosphere, Quail are likely to wander around, laying their eggs at any spot they see fit. This means that you have to exercise great caution while looking for eggs, to avoid damaging any before you collect them. Damage could also be caused by other Quail or animals in your space, so it is crucial that you collect the eggs soon after they are laid' sometimes making about three or four trips around the housing area to check for new eggs.

Quail generally prefer the mid to late hours of the waking day to lay their eggs - between the last hours of afternoon and the early hours of dusk. Therefore, it makes best sense to collect the eggs during the latter half of the day, making your final run around the cage when the Quail have been sent to bed. Ensure that you carry a plastic egg tray to deposit the eggs into, taking care to store the cleaner ones away from those with a dirtier shell.

As you go about collecting your eggs, examine them for cracks, irregularities on the shell or inconsistencies in the appearance. The healthy Quail egg should be as close as possible in appearance to the description of the egg above. The more deformities in the Quail egg, the less it is likely to hatch into a healthy Quilling. This egg examination, therefore, is crucial in case you're planning to start your Quail flock.

All those Quail eggs that pass your critical examination then need to be hygienic and clean. Plenty of unhealthy microbial life is likely to be present on the shells, and if not cleaned away, may seep into the yolk through the tiniest crack on the egg. Your best options to clean the egg without damaging its fragile exterior is to use a piece of steel wool or even a damp cloth. Wipe down your egg gently without applying too much pressure, and do not wash it under any circumstances! Washing has been observed to have negative effects on the hatching process. If you are extremely picky about the hygiene of the eggs, you can also try basic fumigation. Simply wipe down your eggs with a mixture of potassium permanganate and formalin to clean the area of dangerous bacteria.

4. Hatching the Eggs

Should you choose to have your Quail eggs hatch into little chicks, determine the process by which you'd like the hatchlings to emerge. Since Quail are famed for their egg laying abilities, you will receive anywhere between 150 and 200 eggs a year with prolific layer breeds. It may not be possible for your bird to hatch all these eggs by herself successfully. Working with your Quail, you can provide optimum incubation conditions - natural or artificial - to hatch as many healthy chicks as possible.

1. Natural Incubation

The most obvious choice for incubation of your Quail eggs would be through the natural method - having the Quail hatch the eggs herself. In the wild, a female Quail likes to collectively nest and hatch her eggs. To facilitate this, she stops laying eggs at a certain time during the day and prepares herself to physically place herself over the eggs. This process, called brooding, is part of a Quail's daily routine.

To signal that she is ready to brood, a female Quail will let out a peculiar, yet distinct sound, accompanied by a halt in egg-laying. If you have provided a specific nesting zone for your Quail, it is here that she will lay the eggs and then return to brood.

Once the Quail plants herself over this group of eggs, it takes around a week for the hatchlings to begin development. At the end of this week, you can determine whether the egg is fertile by holding it against a bright light source. A fertile egg will have visible matter on the inside, while an infertile one will appear clear.

While this method of natural incubation should be sufficient to hatch most Quail, generations of domesticity have turned many Quail breeds raised in captivity relatively indifferent towards their eggs. Not only do they lay the eggs in a haphazard manner, but also spend little or no time nesting and incubating their clutch.

Should you choose to adopt the natural incubation method for your quail eggs, you may either have to find a hen among the flock who practices nesting and brooding behaviors, encourage nesting habits in the prospective layer hens or introduce a Bantam hen to the flock - a breed of hen that is an avid nester.

2. Artificial Incubation

Brooding is a process undertaken by the Quail when she can find the eggs she has laid during the day. If you collect the Quail's eggs in her absence at the end of each day, her brooding instincts will diminish and even disappear altogether (this may already have become the case with generations of Quail domesticity and husbandry). When you collect the eggs with the purpose of hatching them, however, artificial incubation becomes essential.

The entire process of incubation takes about 18 days, and you can find many commercially manufactured incubators that correctly serve this purpose. Incubating Quail eggs is a tricky procedure that requires specific temperature and humidity settings. Commercial incubators solve this problem by allowing you to regulate conditions with an inbuilt thermostat.

The most interesting feature of artificial incubators is that they allow you to hatch many eggs at once. Since the eggs themselves take around a month to hatch, it is wise to collect many eggs before incubating them together. Quail eggs can keep for approximately ten days before incubation, provided they are stored in the right conditions. Optimum conditions for Quail egg storage are a temperature of 12-17 degrees Celsius 955 degrees Fahrenheit) with a humidity percentage of 75.

Once you have a sufficient number of stored eggs, place them at room temperature for around 6 hours before you shift them into the incubator. This will prepare the eggs for the heightened conditions within the incubating space, which should be set to 37.8 degrees Celsius at humidity percentage of 55 for the first seven days. Towards the end of the incubation process (the last eight days), you should reduce the temperature by 0.3 degrees for optimum hatching. Check for fertilized and developing eggs the same way you would check eggs in the natural incubation method.

Throughout the incubation process, you should turn the eggs at about 90 degrees multiple times every day to prevent the contents from sticking to the shell. In case you have too many eggs and the process is too tedious, you can find equipment that will turn your eggs for you!

5. Caring for newly hatched Quail

Even though you may undertake the incubation process with utmost care and caution, you still should not be disappointed if all the eggs don't hatch. Quail eggs, have a 75 percent rate of hatching, and for a hatchling to successfully emerge from incubation, it has to first be shifted to a brooder.

Brooding zones for hatchlings are critical to their survival, whether they have hatched through the artificial or natural incubation method. You should shift the hatchlings into the brooder almost as soon as they hatch; this brooder can be a commercially manufactured predetermined one, or even a makeshift aquarium or container set up to house hatchlings.

While it is tricky to determine the exact moment of hatching, a Quail mother will signal the hatching period by spending less time sitting on the eggs. When she spends almost no time with the eggs at all, you know they're ready to crack! In an artificial setting, keeping a constant eye on the eggs between the 16th and 18th days will usually reward you with the sight of a hatching quail.

Newborn hatchlings survive best when fed with specially-raised starter diet feed programs, prepared to contain all the necessary nutrients. Tougher forms of food, such as grit, are safe to feed the Quail once they're over six weeks old. They will also need constant sources of clean water placed in shallow bowls, may need to be guided towards water feeders, and will need to be provided with a heating source in the corner of the brooder through a small heating lamp.

There is no hard evidence that advocates one method of hatching over the other. While the natural way seems like the best hatching technique, its low success rate in a captive setting made allowed artificial incubation to meet with great success. The final choice truly comes down your individual settings, preferences and expectations from your flock of Quail.

5. Factors affecting your Quail's egg-laying habits

If you have raised your Quail with the specific purpose of using their eggs, you will, at some point, find differences in the egg-laying habits of your birds. There may be a shift or drop in the frequency, or your Quail may not be laying any eggs at all. In case your Quail has developed certain ailments or reproductive disorders, a check-up with your local expert should help isolate the cause. In many cases, however, several natural and environmental factors may combine to affect the way a perfectly healthy Quail lays their eggs, such as:

1. The age of your bird

Even though Quail may be prolific breeders, their reproductive abilities do diminish as they age, with their egg-laying possibly coming to a full stop in the last stages of their lives.

2. Unfavorable weather conditions

As we have seen, successful egg-laying depends on favorable weather conditions. If the area is not warm enough, or airy enough for the Quail, they will find it difficult to be comfortable enough to lay eggs.

3. Parasites and predators in the environment

If your Quail feel threatened by any predatory sources in their surroundings, they will become highly paranoid and stressed. As a defence mechanism, they may stop laying eggs altogether.

4. Arrival of new flock members

Quail may be sociable to a degree towards humans, but they also possess highly territorial and aggressive natures towards each other. If you introduce new birds to the flock just before the nesting season, you tend to disturb the already established pecking order. Some Quail may then not resume laying eggs until the new birds have been properly integrated into the community and the pecking order has been modified and re-established.

5. Ready to brood

Brooding is perhaps the biggest factor that may cause your Quail to stop laying eggs, but it is often the factor that owners have least knowledge of. If your hens do exhibit nesting and brooding behaviours, they often prefer to lay all their eggs first, and then nest them together at a time. If your bird has suddenly stopped laying eggs, she could just be looking for those that you collected. With time and consistency, Quail adjust to their disappearing eggs and simply lay new ones when they can't find their eggs anymore. Therefore, brooding is a habit that will occur more commonly among newer, younger mothers.

No matter what the causal factor, a sudden slump or halt in laying eggs is not enough to classify your Quail as infertile. It is, in fact, necessary that you reassess your husbandry practices, along with the factors in the Quail's environment thoroughly, to ensure that your Quail receives the kind of care that allow it to lay eggs well past its prime.

6. Maximizing your Quail's egg-laying potential

Once you begin collecting Quail eggs, and see for yourself how much you can gain from either breeding or using the eggs for profit, you may obviously want to yield as many eggs as possible from your layer breeds. Through some easy measures and preparation, you can ensure that your birds provide the most amount of healthy eggs they can.

1. Control the lighting conditions

The most important feature that ensures consistent egg-laying is proper and consistent lighting, especially during the winter months. Quail are the most sexually active during the months of January and June, when the days are relatively longer, and may generally lay few eggs or become sterile for brief periods during the winter months. For the Quail hen to consistently lay throughout the year, she requires about 17 hours of constant light, whether naturally or artificially provided. This is evidently not possible with natural lighting, so you will have to make artificial lighting arrangements.

For artificial lighting arrangements, understand that you cannot increase the Quail's exposure to light by a great amount overnight. You also cannot keep them entirely in light; the birds require a few hours of complete darkness for rest and regeneration. Quail require stable conditions to be comfortable, so increase the exposure to light by about half an hour daily, at the start and end of the day, till you reach 17 hours in a few days' time.

2. Regulate the feed

Along with adequate lighting, the nature of the feed is crucial in determining the frequency and quality of the Quail eggs. There are plenty of food programs available for your Quail on the market today based on its changing nutritional requirements, so be as fussy as you can. Ensure that the feed contains all the vitamins and minerals – especially protein - your birds may need, and that the feed is as fresh as possible. Any bacterial or fungal growth on the feed may adversely affect the bird's health.

Apart from the quality of the feed, you also have to ensure that the feed is appropriate for the type of purpose your Quail serves. Broiler breeds will require different nutritional components in their feed from layer breeds, and layer breeds will need still more protein than other Quail during the moulting season.

A consistency in the supply and frequency of the feed is also essential to help the hens produce eggs that are of optimum condition. Overweight or underweight Quail will probably develop health issues that may obstruct their fertility and reproduction ability. Ideally, 20 gms of feed changed daily should be adequate for your Quail.

3. Keep the Quail roosters to a minimum

Due to the social nature and aggressive mating habits of Quail in captivity, the composition of roosters in proportion to female Quail is crucial in maintaining a peaceful and sexually active environment. Ideally, one rooster is sufficient for a group of 5 female Quail among most breeds such as the Coturnix varieties. Having more females than males may affect the rate of egg-laying, while too many males may mate the females to injury or even death.

4. Stress-free Quail lay the most eggs!

Layer breeds in general, and Quail in particular, are extremely fond of order and calm for a productive egg-laying environment. Their daily routines are determined by a specific amount of food, drink, activity and rest with standardized timings for each activity. Furthermore, Quail are also extremely sensitive to lighting conditions, climatic changes, new locations and even new people. Therefore, maintain as strict a routine as you can with your Quail. The familiarity will put them at ease and allow them to lay eggs in a comfortable and secure space.

The choice to breed and rear Quail for profit is one that requires great commitment, time and patience. To get the most out of your breeding endeavour, it is essential that you immerse yourself into the daily habits of your birds. Once you learn the behaviour and egg-laying patterns of your Quail, the care-taking process becomes easier and comforting, both for you and your birds.

There is plenty of help available, should you require it while breeding your Quail. Different breeds exhibit varying behaviours and may naturally arouse your curiosity from time to time. Do not hesitate to consult your local game bird expert with any queries regarding your Quail, the eggs, or the hatchlings.

Above all, understand that breeding Quail for profit is a process that may not be overly time-consuming, but requires dedication. You have to be extremely patient and diligent in your efforts. As long as you can provide and maintain a healthy and sustained environment for your Quail, you will find this experience to be not only profitable, but also rewarding.

7. The Essential Quail Care Shopping List

The following list comprises all the items you will need to care for your Quail on a daily basis - from housing to diet, including accessories for a cage. Most of these products will be available at your local pet stores, whether in the United States, Canada or the United Kingdom.

Several companies also offer pet accessories for sale through online retail websites. In the United States and Canada, you can access www.petsmart.com to find items that address your quail care needs, while Pets at Home offers the same services in the United Kingdom.

Housing

Cage, preferably bird cage or large aviary (indoor or outdoor)

OR
Chicken coop with run
OR
Rabbit hutch
OR
Aquarium (preferably for smaller Quail)
Brooder
Incubator
Water feeder (1 per pair)
Feeders (1-4, depending on the size of the cage and number of Quail)
Pet-bedding (such as Burgess or ProRep)
Feeding hay for bedding (such as Timothy)
Nest box (1 per Quail)
Pesticides and Insecticides

Accessories
LED Lighting Fixtures
Hiding cubbies
Heating Lamps
Twigs, branches, logs
Perches, swings
Travel carrier (such as Ferplast)

Diet

Fruits and Vegetables
Apples
Blackberries
Blueberries
Loganberries
Cranberries
Boysenberries
Pears
Squash
Pumpkin
Papaya

Grapes
Pineapple
Watermelon
Persimmon
Eggplant
Figs
Peaches
Cucumber
Cantaloupe
Collard Greens
Romaine Lettuce
Raddichio
Carrots
Broccoli
Cauliflower
Cabbage
Asparagus
Kale
Beets
Sprouts

Nuts, Grains, Dried fruit and Seeds
Wheat
Barley
Oats
Cracked corn
Millet
Maize
Rice
Peas

Flowers and plants
Clover
Daisies
Dandelions
Hawthorne
Hibiscus
Wintergrass

Honeysuckle
Rosehips, petals
Magnolia
Marigold

Wheatgrass
Dallis grass
Kikuyu grass
Rye grass
Bermuda grass
Centipedegrass
Blue grass
Fescue grass
Zoysia grass

Live feed
Crickets
Superworms
Waxworms
Silkworms
Earthworms
Nightcrawlers
Wriggler Worms
Mealworms

Nutritional supplements
Oyster shell
Cuttlefish bones

Conclusion

Now that you are equipped with all the information that you need with respect to the Quail, I am sure that you will make a great owner. It is a lot of work to keep Quail at home.

While that may sound intimidating, if you are unable to match all the requirements and needs of your pets, you will only compromise on their health and well-being. To conclude, I would like to remind to that a Quail is a big financial commitment.

Here is a breakdown of the approximate costs of keeping a Quail:

• Cage: $185 to $425 or £120 to £275

• Bedding: $6 to $30 or £4 to £20

• Feed: $4 to $10 or £3 to £7 for a 2 pound bag

• Feeder: $3 to $10 or £52to £7

• Water-feeder: $3 to $10 or £2 to £7

• Nesting box: $20 or £10

• Accessories: $40 to $150 or £20 to £230

Once you are sure of making this commitment, you can convert your home into a great place for your Quail.

I hope this book answers all your questions about having Quail.

References

Seek to continually learn more about your Quail. As with the husbandry of all domestic animals, new techniques and strategies are developed constantly. Never turn down an opportunity to learn more about your new pets, and eagerly seek out those who may know more than you do about these big, beautiful birds.

Books

Naturalized Birds of the World
By Christopher Lever   A&C Black 2010

Diseases of Poultry

Edited by David E. Swayne

John Wiley & Sons, 2013

Biology of Breeding Poultry

By Paul M. Hocking   CABI, 2009

Keeping Quail: A Guide to Domestic and Commercial Management

Katie Thear

Practical Quail-keeping

Sarah Barratt

Websites

In the information age, learning more about your Quail is only a few clicks away. Be sure to bookmark these sites for quick access in the future.

Important: At the time of writing, all the following links were active and functional; in the event that any source should re-direct you to an inactive page, please understand that the maintenance of these websites is subject to Internet-policies and the preferences of the website owners; we cannot claim personal responsibility for the same.

Informational Websites

Backyard Chickens

www.backyardchickens.com

Though focused on chickens, this website and message board contains plenty of information about Quail care as well.

Poultry Hub

www.poultryhub.org

Maintained by the Poultry Cooperative Research Centre, Poultry Hub provides information regarding all aspects of Quail care.

Birding Information

www.birdinginformation.com

Birding Information provides extensive knowledge on several types of birds, including the various breeds of Quail.

UK Farming Guidelines Section

www.gov.uk

This site includes information on the farming, housing and husbandry guidelines for Quail and other types of poultry.

Backyard Poultry

www.backyardpoultrymag.com

Online magazine featuring news, information and more concerning Quail and other common poultry.

Cornell Lab of Ornithology

www.birds.cornell.edu

Information about most birds native to North America. This site provides identification photos, sample calls from most species and tips for spotting various species in the wild.

The Poultry Club of Great Britain

www.poultryclub.org

This website provides a variety of helpful resources, as well as information about poultry husbandry and breeding. You can also use this website to find information on breed standards, competitions and meet other poultry enthusiasts.

Xeno-Canto

www.xeno-canto.org

Based in the Netherlands, xeno-canto is a repository for birds sounds, collected from around the world.

Beauty of Birds

www.beautyofbirds.com

Beauty of Birds has information on Quail, including data about wild colonies, behavioural patterns, etc.

The Bird Hotline

www.birdhotline.com

A wealth of information is available on this site. While most is oriented towards parakeets and similar birds, the veterinary resources provided on the website are of value to Quail keepers.

Breeders

Quail breeders are not only an excellent source for purchasing hatchlings; they can also provide a wealth of information through detailed and interactive forums posted on the Internet.

Cheap Chicks Poultry Farm

www.cheapchickpoultryfarm.weebly.com

Cheap Chicks Poultry Farm sells hatchlings and eggs of Quail and many other poultry breeds.

Metzer Farms

www.metzerfarms.com

Metzer Farms hatches a variety of bird species, and their website provides information about Quail housing, maintenance and feeding.

University and Governmental Resources
University of Texas at El Paso

www.utep.edu

The University of Texas, El Paso website contains a great deal of Quail-oriented information. Of special note are the bird taxonomy resources, which provide information about the classification of Quails.

University of California, Davis

www.animalscience.ucdavis.edu

UC Davis works extensively with livestock (including poultry), and they work to enhance the lives of captive and companion animals through science.

The Poultry Site

www.thepoultrysite.com

Although primarily focused on turkeys and chickens, this Oklahoma State University maintained website contains some information about Quail.

Animal Diversity Web

www.animaldiversity.ummz.umich.edu

Maintained by the University of Michigan, the Animal Diversity Web has thousands of pages of information, detailing the lives of various animal species. In addition to reading about Quail, you can also learn about their predators, prey and competitors here.

Centre for Integrated Agricultural Systems

www.cias.wisc.edu

This page, provided and maintained by the University of Wisconsin-Madison, contains a wealth of data concerning all common farm animals, including Quail.

The Centres for Disease Control and Prevention

www.cdc.gov

Based in Atlanta, Georgia, the CDC provides information on a variety of diseases that may be zoonotic. Additionally, the website provides further resources for coping with outbreaks of salmonella.

Veterinary Resources

Veterinarians.com

www.localvets.com

This site is a search engine that can help you find a local veterinarian to treat your Quail.

European Committee of the Association of Avian Veterinarians

http://www.eaavonline.org/

This website includes a veterinarian locator, as well as a long list of links that may be useful for Quail owners.

All About Birds

www.allaboutbirds.org

A comprehensive website that covers various subjects like life history, care and breeding of different domestic birds.

AvianBiotech.com

www.avianbiotech.com

AvianBiotech.com provides DNA-based lab services to bird owners.

Association of Avian Veterinarians

http://www.aav.org/

In addition to being a good resource for finding a qualified avian veterinarian, this site provides information on veterinary colleges, bird health and basic care.

For The Birds

www.forthebirdsdvm.com

Veterinary and care information for all birds, as well as specific care advice for Quail.

Published by IMB Publishing 2015